BODYGUARDS!

From GLADIATORS to the SECRET SERVICE

ED BUTTS

ART BY SCOTT PLUMBE

annick press
toronto + new york + vancouver

Edited by Kathy Lowinger
Copyedited by Tanya Trafford
Designed by Natalie Olsen, Kisscut Design

Annick Press Ltd.

We acknowledge the support of the Canada Council for the Arts, the Ontario Arts Council, and the Government of Canada through the Canada Book Fund (CBF) for our publishing activities.

ONTARIO ARTS COUNCIL
CONSEIL DES ARTS DE L'ONTARIO

Cataloging in Publication
Butts, Edward, 1951–
Bodyguards! : from gladiators to the Secret Service / Ed Butts
; art by Scott Plumbe.

Includes bibliographical references and index.
ISBN 978-1-55451-437-3 (bound). — ISBN 978-1-55451-436-6 (pbk.)

1. Bodyguards—History—Juvenile literature.
I. Plumbe, Scott
II. Title.

HV8290.B88 2012   j363.28'9   C2012-901489-3

Distributed in Canada by:
Firefly Books Ltd.
66 Leek Crescent
Richmond Hill, ON
L4B 1H1

Published in the U.S.A. by Annick Press (U.S.) Ltd.
Distributed in the U.S.A. by:
Firefly Books (U.S.) Inc.
P.O. Box 1338   Ellicott Station
Buffalo, NY 14205

Printed in China

Visit us at: www.annickpress.com
Visit Scott Plumbe at: www.scottplumbe.com

CONTENTS

INTRODUCTION
ON GUARD FOR YOU 1

CHAPTER 1
THE FIRST BODYGUARDS 3

CHAPTER 2
THE HALLS OF POWER 25

CHAPTER 3
BAD GUYS AND GUNMEN 45

CHAPTER 4
WHEN BODYGUARDS FAIL OR BETRAY 59

CHAPTER 5
THE HIGH PRICE OF FAME 75

CHAPTER 6
ON ASSIGNMENT 83

CHAPTER 7
SO YOU WANT TO BE A BODYGUARD 101

CONCLUSION
DEBRIEF 113

Glossary 114
Bodyguard Timeline 116
Bibliography 118
Index 119
Image Credits 121
About the Author and Illustrator 122

FOR MY GRANDSON, AUSTIN JAMES BUTTS — E.B.

FOR MY PARENTS, ON GUARD FROM DAY ONE — S.P.

ACKNOWLEDGMENTS

Thank you to Ali Sikandar Hayat of the International Association of Personal Protection Agents (IAPPA) and Shawn Engbrecht of the Center for Advanced Security Studies. Also Kathy Lowinger, Tanya Trafford, and Annick Press. My thanks too, as always, to the staff of the Guelph Public Library.

nations. The Immortals were at the head of a Persian army of more than two hundred thousand men that had invaded Greece. King Xerxes sat high on a hilltop so he could watch his Immortals crush the Greeks.

On the other side was a Greek army of about five thousand men. They were led by Leonidas, king of Sparta, one of the independent city-states that made up Greece. On the frontlines of the Greek army were three hundred Spartan soldiers, King Leonidas's personal bodyguard. It looked as though the Greeks were hopelessly outnumbered. But Leonidas's bodyguards were not ordinary soldiers. They had been preparing all their lives for a day just like this one.

NO LOSERS ALLOWED!

The Spartans held fierce competitions to choose the bravest and most skilled warriors for the king's bodyguard. The winners were the best of the best. When the warriors marched off to war, Spartan women would call out to them, "Come home with your shield, or on it." In other words, victory or death!

The Spartans had the best army in ancient Greece, because they believed that nothing was more important than military strength. School for Spartan boys was brutal. To make them tough, they were beaten, starved, and exposed to every kind of hardship imaginable. They had to endure pain silently. Even some of their food was so awful that nobody but a Spartan could eat it.

Spartan boys learned how to fight with spears and short, razor-sharp swords. Most important, they were trained to keep in close formation on the battlefield and fight as a single unit. They would stand shoulder to shoulder, so that their shields of wood, leather, and bronze made a solid defensive wall.

NOW THEY STOOD OUTNUMBERED AT THERMOPYLAE
but the Spartan royal bodyguards were prepared to defend all
of Greece. A Persian officer demanded that the Spartans surrender
their weapons. Leonidas defiantly replied, "Come and get them!"
Then the battle was on.

For two days, Leonidas and the royal bodyguards held the
pass. There was no room for the Persians to take advantage of their
greater numbers. Watching from the hilltop, Xerxes was stunned
to see that his famous Immortals were no match for the Spartans.

Then a Greek traitor showed the Persians a secret path
through the mountains. The Persians would be able to get around
behind the Greek army and attack it from both the front and
the rear. When Leonidas realized that his army was going to
be surrounded, he ordered most of the Greek warriors to retreat
so they wouldn't all be killed. However, he and his bodyguard
stayed, along with a few other volunteers, so they could give
the rest of the Greek army time to escape.

The fighting was furious as thousands of Immortals closed
in on the small band of Spartans. Leonidas was killed, but his
men still refused to surrender. Finally, only a few of the Spartan
bodyguards were left. The Persians finished them off with
volleys of arrows.

The Spartans' courageous stand at Thermopylae inspired
the rest of the Greeks to resist the Persian invasion. They
defeated the Persians in later battles, and Xerxes had to with-
draw his army from Greece. Today, a statue of Leonidas marks
the place where he and his bodyguards fought to the last man.

Even though the Persians had failed to conquer Greece,
they still ruled the most powerful empire in the world. Many
years after the death of Leonidas, another Greek king led his
army on a bold invasion of the Persian Empire. He was Alexander
of Macedon. History books would refer to him as Alexander
the Great.

ALEXANDER WAS A BRILLIANT GENERAL. Though he won victory after victory over Persian armies, he knew he had enemies everywhere, even among his followers. His own father, King Philip II of Macedon, had been killed by an assassin. Alexander was skilled with weapons and vain enough to think nobody could beat him in a fight. But he was also smart enough to realize that he needed the protection of bodyguards.

Alexander was a fearless leader who personally led his men into battle on horseback. He was always in the thick of the fighting. The white plume on his helmet and his dazzling armor made him stand out as a target for the enemy. It was as though he was daring them to try to kill him. To get at Alexander, enemy soldiers would have had to fight their way through his royal bodyguard—a superb cavalry unit called the Companions.

The Companions were noblemen who were expert riders and fought from the saddle with spears and swords. Every one of them was sworn to defend Alexander with his life. But as a fighting king, Alexander knew that in the heat and confusion of battle, almost anything could happen. For extra protection, he chose seven officers from the Companions to be his closest personal bodyguards. These were the men he considered the most trustworthy and loyal. They had their work cut out for them.

In one raging battle, a bodyguard named Clietus saw a Persian soldier knock Alexander down with a battle-ax. Alexander had lost his helmet and was on the ground, dazed and defenseless. But before the Persian could strike at Alexander's unprotected head, Clietus hurled his spear and killed the attacker.

Clietus didn't know it, but the moment he saved Alexander's life was a turning point in history. Alexander went on to become ruler of the largest empire the ancient world had ever known. He spread Greek culture all the way to India. Had Clietus been too slow, or if he had missed, the history of the world would have been very different.

Unfortunately for Clietus, Alexander had a bad temper, especially after too much wine. One night Alexander and his bodyguards were all drinking heavily. Foolishly, Clietus insulted Alexander to his face. In a fit of drunken rage, Alexander grabbed a spear from another bodyguard and ran Clietus through with it, killing him on the spot. Alexander later said he was sorry for what he had done, but the bodyguards began to wonder if he was going mad.

Alexander the Great didn't live long enough to enjoy being master of his enormous empire. At the age of thirty-two, he caught a fever and died. As he lay on his deathbed with his bodyguards surrounding him, one of them asked Alexander who would inherit his empire. Alexander replied that it should go "to the strongest." His bodyguards divided up the empire and made themselves kings.

WARRIOR WOMEN

Chandragupta Maurya, a ruler who conquered much of the Indian subcontinent, believed that women were more trustworthy than men. Many of his personal bodyguard of over five hundred highly trained female warriors were said to be Greek women who had followed the army of Alexander the Great.

GLADIATORS AND THE PRAETORIAN GUARD OF ROME

TWO THOUSAND YEARS AGO Rome was one of the richest and most powerful cities in the world, but it could be a dangerous place to live. Most of its wealth and power was in the hands of a very small ruling class called patricians. The lower class plebeians were poor. Even those who had work didn't always make enough to survive. They had to beg or steal to feed their families. In some neighborhoods, criminal gangs forced the residents, the merchants, and even people just passing through to pay for protection—from *them*. Children were often snatched from the streets and sold into slavery.

To walk the streets of Rome safely, if you could afford it, you needed a bodyguard. And everybody knew who made the best bodyguards: gladiators.

Romans had bloodthirsty tastes when it came to entertainment. They went to the arena to watch gladiators fight, sometimes to the death. Some gladiators had been enemy soldiers, captured in battle. Others were convicted criminals, or men who had been forced to sell themselves into slavery because they owed money. A handful of them were free men who simply loved the thrill of fighting in the arena. There were even female gladiators.

Gladiators were trained in special schools to fight with a variety of weapons: swords, daggers, spears, nets, and long forks called tridents. The training was brutal, and many would-be gladiators were killed or seriously injured before they even stepped into the arena. But if a slave survived training and became a gladiator, he became a valuable piece

of property for his owner. He was well fed and given a comfortable place to sleep, much like a prized racehorse of today.

While no respectable citizen would invite a gladiator to dinner, Romans admired gladiators the way people today admire star athletes. Gladiators were strong, skilled fighters, but the best gladiators only fought in the arena a few times a year when special games were held. Between games, their owners rented them out as bodyguards. For a patrician, having a gladiator or two for protection was a status symbol. The more famous the gladiator was, the more his services would cost. A generous owner would even let the gladiator keep some of the money.

Gladiators were very effective bodyguards. Unlike other slaves, they were allowed to carry weapons when they were on duty. If you were a man on your way to the forum, a woman going to a party, or a child off to buy cakes at the bakery, you wouldn't have to worry about thieves, beggars, or street ruffians if you were being escorted by a well-known killing machine.

Your gladiator bodyguard would also be good at clearing a way for you through dirty, crowded, narrow streets.

One problem for gladiator owners: the day after the games, a patrician would often find that his favorite gladiator was no longer available. Even the best gladiators didn't live very long. Most of those who fought in the arena died there.

ANCIENT ROME'S MOST FAMOUS BODYGUARDS were the Praetorian Guards. Originally, the Praetorians had guarded generals like Julius Caesar and Marc Antony. Then the first Roman emperor, Caesar Augustus, made them his official imperial guard. The Praetorians protected the emperor's palace, and they escorted the emperor wherever he went.

They were armed with spears, because no one was allowed to have a sword or dagger in the emperor's presence. Swords and daggers could be hidden in clothing. If a Praetorian caught you with a weapon, you'd become food for the lions in the arena.

Members of the Praetorian Guard were paid better than regular soldiers, and they got to live in Rome rather than a remote army camp, so any Roman soldier would have wanted to be one. However, only the best soldiers were chosen. The Praetorians were easy to recognize because of their oval shields and special badges. When they marched through the streets of Rome, everyone got out of the way.

The Praetorian Guard became a powerful force in Rome. Emperors gave Praetorian officers large gifts of money to ensure their loyalty. They had reason to be nervous. If the Praetorians didn't like an emperor, they might just get rid of him. Caligula was one of Rome's cruelest emperors: at a sporting event he once ordered that a section of the crowd be thrown into the arena to be eaten by wild animals— just because he was bored. Needless to say, his behavior turned many people against him. He eventually made the mistake of insulting his Praetorian Guards. One day, as Caligula was walking through a tunnel that led from the arena to his palace, his bodyguards suddenly turned on him. They stabbed him to death.

The most famous Praetorian Guard was Sempronius Densus. He refused to join his fellow bodyguards in a plot to assassinate the emperor Galba. Instead, he fought to the death trying to defend Galba, who was also killed. Because of his courage and loyalty, Romans saw Sempronius Densus as the model of what an imperial bodyguard should be.

THE SAMURAI OF JAPAN: THOSE WHO SERVE

JAPAN HAD AN EMPEROR, but he was a figurehead without any real power. Political and military power was in the hands of warlords called *shoguns*, who owned vast estates. Right below the shoguns on the social ladder were noblemen called *daimyos*. Daimyos ran the shoguns' estates and were the highest rank of *samurai*, a class of fierce warriors who held much power in Japan for a thousand years. The word samurai means "those who serve." The rest of the samurai were professional warriors dedicated to the daimyos and shoguns they served. They were their masters' bodyguards. If there were enough of them, they even made up their masters' armies.

A samurai was given a farm to produce food for him and his family, but he didn't do any of the farming himself. That kind of work was beneath him and was done by peasants. A samurai's only job was to serve and protect his master, and he was superb at it.

Samurai should not be confused with *ninja*, a fourteenth-century secret order of spies and assassins trained in martial arts who offered their services to the highest bidder.

A samurai warrior's training began when he was three years old, using a wooden sword. At the age of thirteen he began practicing with real weapons. Samurai used the bow and arrow, a spear called a *yari*, and a *naginata*, which was a long pole with a curved blade at the end. Samurai became best known for fighting with the *katana*, the famous samurai sword. In the hands of a skilled swordsman, a long, razor-edged katana was a frighteningly efficient weapon.

Even after gunpowder was introduced to Japan, and samurai began to use firearms, the katana remained their symbol. The sword was called "the soul of the samurai," and no true warrior was ever without it.

Samurai also had to be excellent horsemen. They learned how to shoot arrows from the saddle while the horse was in full gallop. They didn't use shields, but they did wear armor. A samurai's helmet was designed to look terrifying and was sometimes worn with a mask that gave the samurai a face like a demon.

A samurai was the ultimate bodyguard—a warrior who had to be ready to die for his master. Anything less would bring disgrace upon him. Rather than live in shame, a samurai who had failed in his duty would compose a death poem, and then take his own life in a ritual called *seppuku*. A samurai master had the responsibility of rewarding warriors for their courage and faithfulness. A warlord who neglected his protectors would regret it, as they could abandon him and become *ronin*, samurai without a master.

HONOR BOUND

There was more to the samurai way of life than violence. They believed in a code of honor called *bushido*. This code required the samurai to always seek enlightenment and understanding. Besides being deadly protectors of their masters, samurai loved art, music, and poetry, and appreciated the beauty of nature.

For many generations, Japan was torn by warfare as rival shoguns fought for land and power. Japanese history and legend is full of stories about samurai heroes. One of the most famous stories is about a daimyo named Asano who quarreled with a powerful shogun official named Kira. Asano scratched Kira with his knife. For this insult, Asano was obliged to commit seppuku, and his lands were seized.

Forty-seven of Asano's samurai, who were now without a master, spent two years planning to avenge Asano's death. Once they felt prepared, they attacked Kira's castle. They killed the shogun and dutifully placed his head on Asano's grave. Then the ronin turned themselves in to the authorities and were ordered to perform the ritual suicide. But because of their devotion to their master, even after he was dead, these men were regarded as heroes who represented samurai honor. Today, their gravesite is a Japanese national shrine and a monument to bodyguards who were loyal to the end.

CHAPTER

THE HALLS OF POWER

MANY PEOPLE DREAM ABOUT what it would be like to be a king or a queen, or the president of a country. Imagine having the power to make everybody around you carry out your every wish. But having power has its dark side. If you're the leader, it's hard to tell who your friends are and who just wants to get close to you to win your favor. Others will disagree with your decisions. Worse, history is full of stories about leaders who were the victims of assaults, kidnappings, and even assassinations. As long as there have been people in power, there have been bodyguards to help them hold onto that power and to protect them—sometimes even after they are dead.

King Henry VIII and the British monarchs who succeeded him were protected by bodyguards known as the Honourable Band of Gentleman Pensioners. The word "pensioner" had nothing to do with age. It meant that their position entitled them to a pension paid by the Crown.

BODYGUARDS FOR ETERNITY: THE TERRA COTTA ARMY

QIN (PRONOUNCED CHIN) SHI HUANGDI, who lived from 259 to 210 BCE, is known in China as the First Emperor. He was the leader who conquered the lands of independent warlords and united China into one country. In fact, China is named after him.

Qin was one of history's great builders. He put hundreds of thousands of laborers to work building the Great Wall, to protect China from invaders. He created a vast private park for hunting and pleasure. He ordered that a fine palace be built as his home. And early in his reign he commissioned a magnificent tomb. It was a huge project that took years to complete. The tomb itself was a pyramid-shaped artificial hill, 120 meters (393 feet) high. It was surrounded by temples, storehouses, and stables. The entire complex was enclosed by a 6-kilometer (3.7 mile) wall. Anyone who got inside the wall risked setting off booby traps, such as crossbows armed with deadly arrows.

THE FIRST EMPEROR WAS A CRUEL, HARSH MAN— people who offended him were beheaded or buried alive. Not surprisingly, there were several attempts on his life. One man came to the palace bearing a gift—a box containing the head of an enemy. He was brought into the presence of the First Emperor. Suddenly he pulled out a dagger. While the courtiers looked on in shock, Qin ducked behind a column and tried to draw his sword, but it got tangled up in his robes. The attacker chased the First Emperor around and around the column. Finally, the court physician hit the would-be assassin with his medicine bag. That gave the

First Emperor time to free his sword. He stabbed the assailant in the leg. The rest of the courtiers pounced on the wounded man and killed him.

After that, Qin took extraordinary steps to protect himself. His guards' barracks in the palace were placed near his own living quarters. As he moved through his great palace, he would not tell anyone where he was going, or where he would be at any particular time. That way no one could be sure just where he was. It was also forbidden for anyone to repeat anything the First Emperor said. To do so would cost the offender his head. To the people who worked in the palace, it was almost as though the First Emperor was a phantom who saw and heard everything. Their fear of him was an important part of his extra defenses.

His private park was out of bounds. It was guarded by convicted criminals whose lives had been spared in exchange for keeping trespassers out. These guards patrolled the park to protect the wildlife from poachers, and to make sure the First Emperor had privacy while he hunted and entertained the nobles with great feasts. Peasants seldom dared set foot in the park because they knew they faced death if they were caught by the human guards, or by the dragons said to be on patrol along with them.

Qin had bodyguards to protect him from trespassers and attackers, but there was only one thing the all-powerful First Emperor was afraid of: death. His magicians were constantly at work searching for potions and spells that would make him immortal. He was determined that if the day came that he had to be taken to his great tomb, he would one day rise again. And while he was entombed, he wanted protection.

WHEN THE FIRST EMPEROR FINALLY DIED and was laid to rest, his son had everyone who had worked on the tomb killed. That way, nobody alive would know the layout of the tomb compound. But someone decided that even more protection was necessary. Someone of Qin's majesty needed a special, magical army that would last forever. Nobody knows if the idea came from the First Emperor or from his son, but the First Emperor got his unusual army. The modern world would know nothing about it until 1974.

Over the centuries, the mound that marks the site of the First Emperor's tomb had eroded to half its original height. One day, some farmers who were digging a well near Xi'an (*shee-an*), not far from the mound, made an amazing discovery: the head of a life-sized sculpture of a man.

FEARFUL OF ASSASSINS, QIN TRIED EVERYTHING TO EXTEND HIS LIFE...

IN 1974, CHINESE FARMERS DISCOVERED EMPEROR QIN'S LONG-BURIED SECRET—

... FROM DEADLY GUARDS ...

... TO MAGIC POTIONS.

—AN IMMORTAL TERRA COTTA ARMY CREATED TO PROTECT HIM IN DEATH.

The farmers reported their find. Extensive excavations around the tomb revealed one of the most astounding archaeological finds ever: the Terra Cotta Army!

To protect the First Emperor for eternity, artisans created an army of soldiers made from terra cotta, a type of red clay used for making pottery. From what's been found so far, Qin's deathly army of bodyguards numbers over a thousand terra cotta soldiers, but it is estimated that the total number could be eight thousand. The army even has horses and chariots. Every figure is unique. No two faces are the same, but each one looks like an authentic soldier from his hairstyle to the soles of his sandals. They were originally brightly painted, though little of the paint remains. At one time the warriors each held real weapons—spears, swords, and crossbows. But most of the weapons were stolen by the flesh and blood soldiers of later emperors.

When the First Emperor finally went to his tomb, it was for good. The tomb still lies under the huge mound and has never been excavated. But the story of the First Emperor lives on, thanks to his incredible Terra Cotta Army.

BURIED ALIVE

In this period in China's history, when an important leader died, he didn't go to the grave alone. Servants, wives, soldiers, and even nobles were buried with him. Alive! Their duty was to serve and protect their master in the next life.

THE ENGLISH CIVIL WAR WAS FOUGHT BETWEEN THE ARMIES OF KING CHARLES I AND PARLIAMENT. IN ONE BATTLE, THE KING'S SONS, FOURTEEN-YEAR-OLD PRINCE CHARLES AND NINE-YEAR-OLD PRINCE JAMES, WERE ALMOST CAPTURED BY ENEMY SOLDIERS. YOUNG CHARLES PULLED OUT A PISTOL AND CRIED, "I FEAR THEM NOT!" HE DIDN'T HAVE TO USE IT BECAUSE A ROYAL BODYGUARD CALLED PENSIONER WILLIAM RODE TO THE RESCUE. HE STRUCK DOWN AN ENEMY SOLDIER WITH HIS SWORD, AND THEN ESCORTED THE PRINCES TO SAFETY.

THE DAHOMEY MINOS: THE KING'S AMAZONS

IN THE EIGHTEENTH CENTURY, the kingdom of Dahomey (now Benin), in west-central Africa, was ravaged by the notorious slave trade. So many men were carried off by slavers that there were few people left in Dahomey to serve in the king's army. The king decided that if he was going to have a strong army, he'd have to include women as warriors.

Many of the women were volunteers who wanted to be warriors, but some were forced into the king's service because their husbands or fathers disapproved of the way they'd behaved.

These female soldiers were called the *Minos*, which means "mothers." But they proudly boasted, "We are men, not women," and in many ways were treated equally, although they were kept separate from the men and not allowed to marry.

They were trained to fight with muskets, clubs, spears, knives, and swords. The ones who were the best sword-fighters were called *nyekplo-hen-to*, which means "razor women." A company of archers made up of the youngest women fired barbed, poisoned arrows.

The Minos proved to be brave and fierce fighters. In one battle against a neighboring tribe, when the male Dahomey warriors fled from the enemy, the Minos stood their ground. The king was so impressed that he added Minos fighters to his royal bodyguard. These Minos were called *ahosi*, "the king's wives." They lived in their own barracks on the palace grounds. When they were not at war or guarding the king, they spent their time training. Everyone who saw the Minos in action was impressed with their strength and discipline. A British officer who had observed the Minos training noted in his report, "On a campaign, I would prefer the women of that country, as soldiers, to the men."

Several of the Minos became legendary. Nausica was the king's favorite bodyguard. She was famous both as a dancer and a warrior. She died a hero in battle against the French in 1890, when Africa was being colonized by European powers.

THE VATICAN SWISS GUARD: PROTECTORS OF THE POPE

THE VATICAN IS A TINY, INDEPENDENT STATE in the middle of the city of Rome. For many centuries it has been a place of great importance because it is the home of the pope and the headquarters of the Roman Catholic Church. There was a time when the pope was not only a religious leader. He also had authority over kings and ruled a large part of Italy. At times, rulers of other countries thought that they could increase their own power if they controlled the pope. Therefore, the pope needed extra protection.

In 1506, Pope Julius II hired a company of 150 Swiss mercenaries as his bodyguard. Mercenaries are professional soldiers who fight for anyone who will pay them, rather than for their own country. The Swiss soldiers were known for their courage, their fighting skills, and their strong sense of loyalty to the pope. The pope made them the official "Defenders of the Church's Freedom." That was the beginning of the famous Vatican Swiss Guard.

Those were very troubled times. Everybody wanted the riches that lay to the East—the spices, the precious jewels, and the gorgeous silks. Italian city-states like the Republic of Venice and the Kingdom of Naples fought over who would control the trade for those riches. What's more, the powerful families who ruled France, Spain, and the Holy Roman Empire plotted to seize a share of the trade for themselves.

All sides wanted the pope's support, even if they had to get it by force. The Swiss Guard had to be vigilant in protecting the pope from all these potential enemies. In 1527, the army of Holy Roman Emperor Charles V invaded Rome, planning to capture Pope Clement VII. While an escort of 40 Guards helped the pope escape from the city, a company of 189 others battled the invaders. Only 42 of those Swiss Guards survived. You can still see the site of this historic battle, near St. Peter's Basilica.

The Swiss Guard is still the pope's official bodyguard today. You can see them on duty in the Vatican, and you can have your picture taken with them. They hold medieval weapons and on special occasions wear a metal helmet called a *morion*, decorated with an ostrich feather (at other times they wear a plain beret). Despite the colorful uniforms, the Swiss Guards aren't just there for show. They are trained professionals who watch for any threat or sign of trouble. In addition to the guards you see in uniform, there are others in plainclothes who mix with the crowds of tourists. When the pope travels outside the Vatican, members of the Swiss Guard in plainclothes go with him.

Today's Swiss Guards still come from the same part of Switzerland as the original company of soldiers did. To be eligible to join the Guard, a man must be unmarried, Catholic, and between the ages of nineteen and thirty. (At present, female applicants are not accepted.) He must meet tough physical requirements and must have already completed basic training with the Swiss Army. The Swiss Guard is commanded by a colonel, who is appointed by the pope. New Guards are sworn in every May 6, the anniversary of the Swiss Guards' heroic stand during Emperor Charles V's attack on Rome.

GUARDING IN STYLE

Although widely rumored to have been created by Renaissance artist Michelangelo, the modern Swiss Guard uniform was actually designed in 1914 by Commandant Jules Repond. He is said to have been inspired by the colorful frescoes of Michelangelo's rival Raphael.

THE SS: GUARDIANS OF EVIL

FROM 1933 UNTIL 1945, the dictator Adolf Hitler ruled Germany. He was the leader of the Nazis, a political party that enforced very extreme and cruel policies. Hitler and the Nazis governed through brute force and terror. Anyone who disagreed with them was either executed or sent to a concentration camp, a type of prison. The Nazis' ambitions didn't stop at home. When they sent German armies out to conquer most of Europe, the Nazis ignited World War II.

With all of his evil schemes, Hitler made a lot of enemies, so of course he had bodyguards. In fact, Hitler had thousands of bodyguards. The biggest Nazi security organization was called the *Schutzstaffel* or Shield Squadron—the dreaded SS. And within the SS was an elite group called the Adolf Hitler

Bodyguard. Its members were fanatically devoted to Hitler. Everybody, even German generals, lived in fear of them.

The SS, commanded by Heinrich Himmler, was not part of the regular German military. It was more like Hitler's private army and was responsible for some of the worst crimes committed by the Nazis. Between 1933 and 1945, the SS rounded up millions of Jews, Roma, and other people the Nazis hated and sent them to death camps. Among the dead were more than a million children.

In an incident called The Night of the Long Knives, the SS arrested and murdered more than 170 Germans whom Hitler considered a threat. Some of them had even been his supporters.

Most SS recruits started out as boys in the Hitler Youth. That organization taught children that Hitler was Germany's great *Führer* (leader) and must be obeyed. Boys who graduated to the SS underwent intense physical and military training. They spent long hours doing calisthenics and learning how to use firearms. When a recruit was accepted into the SS, he was given a black uniform with skull and lightning bolt badges. By that time he was a firm believer in Hitler and the Nazis.

A member of the SS had to be able to prove that all his ancestors had been German. He had to place his loyalty to Hitler above loyalty to anyone else, including his family. If he heard anyone, even his own parents, say anything critical of Hitler, he had to report them, even though it meant that they would likely be arrested and taken to a concentration camp.

Even though Hitler was surrounded by bodyguards, there were many plots to assassinate him. One attempt to kill Hitler with a bomb almost succeeded. He escaped with only slight injuries. Hitler owed his life as much to luck as to his bodyguards. That luck ran out as the Nazi armies were defeated by American, British, Canadian, Russian and other Allied nations' armed forces. When Hitler realized that Germany had lost the war, he committed suicide, as did Heinrich Himmler. Many of the SS bodyguards were tried as war criminals and then executed or sent to prison.

THE UNITED STATES SECRET SERVICE: PROTECTING THE PRESIDENT

ON SEPTEMBER 5, 1975, Secret Service Agent Larry M. Buendorf was one of the bodyguards escorting President Gerald Ford through a crowd of people. Suddenly he saw a woman point a gun at the president's head. Buendorf's hand shot out in a flash. He grabbed the pistol, jamming his thumb between the hammer and the firing pin. As long as his thumb was there, the gun couldn't be fired. Bodyguards subdued the woman, Lynette "Squeaky" Fromme, while others hustled President Ford away to safety.

The U.S. Secret Service is one of the most famous bodyguard organizations in the world. The agents of the Secret Service protect the president, the vice-president, presidential candidates, former presidents, and their families. They also protect visiting heads of state and foreign diplomats.

You have probably seen Secret Service agents on the news. They are the people in dark suits and sunglasses who walk alongside the president's car during a motorcade. But they're not the only bodyguards on duty. You probably wouldn't notice the bodyguards wearing ordinary clothes who move through the crowds of people cheering the president, watching for any signs of trouble. In fact, every moment of the day and night, the president is under the careful watch of the Secret Service. They guard his residence, his office, and every place he visits. They even inspect his food in case someone should try to poison him.

All U.S. Secret Service agents are American citizens. Agents attend a special training center outside Washington, D.C., where they are instructed in firearms marksmanship, use of force and control tactics, and emergency medical techniques. All have undergone full background investigations.

As the attempt on President Ford's life showed, being in an outdoor crowd can be dangerous for the president. But the hardest part of a Secret Service agent's job is protecting the president when he is traveling from place to place. Potential assassins or kidnappers could be almost anywhere. That's why the men and women of the Secret Service must scout every route the president is going to take, looking for possible trouble spots. Everything must be carefully timed and there must be a strict schedule in place, so that every agent knows precisely where to be at a given time, and what he or she is supposed to be doing. The plans for such operations are tightly guarded secrets, to avoid information falling into the wrong hands. Every person involved must pass a rigorous security check and even the most determined would-be attacker would have a hard time discovering details that could be used to breach the president's safety.

The driver of the president's car has the skill and training to respond to any sort of emergency. In fact, the drivers of all of the cars in the presidential motorcade know exactly what to do to protect the president in the event of an attack. What if an unauthorized vehicle approaches the motorcade? Immediately, designated Secret Service agents will take the offensive to intercept and stop the vehicle while others clear a route in front

of the president's car so his driver can quickly whisk him away to safety.

If the president were to pay a visit to your school, much of the Secret Service agents' work would be done in advance. They would check out the school carefully. Where would the president enter and what areas would he visit? How many doors and how many windows are there? What about driveways on or off the property? When is the building locked? Who has keys? Alarm codes? The agents would work with local police and the school's administration to make sure that the president and all of the people who would be there to see him stayed safe.

On the day of the visit, agents and police would patrol the school grounds and nearby streets and parks ahead of time. There would be a limit to the number of people allowed in the room in which the president was speaking. You probably wouldn't be able to bring in your backpack or any bags or packages. Everything, including lockers, would be searched carefully. All of these precautions are taken because the Secret Service is not only guarding the president. They're guarding you, too.

CHAPTER

3

BAD GUYS AND GUNMEN

YOU'VE BEEN LOOKING FORWARD TO your birthday
party all year. To remind your friends, you send out a notice
on the Internet. To your shock, you discover that the message
has gone out to dozens and dozens of kids you don't know
and they're planning to crash the party. Then you find out
that some of these party crashers belong to street gangs. You
and your parents call the police. They arrive on the scene to
turn the uninvited guests away, and you've ducked a disaster.

Most of us can assume that when a crime's been committed—or even *may* be committed—the police will be there
to help to keep us and our property safe. We count on the law
because we live our lives more or less according to the law.

But what if you lived in a world without laws? What sort
of extra defenses would you need if you were an outlaw,
living just like the word says, outside the law? Who could
you turn to for protection? Your bodyguard would have the
unusual responsibility of protecting you not only from other
criminals, but also from the police, who might try to arrest
you for breaking the law. In this topsy-turvy situation, it can
be impossible to tell the good guys from the bad guys.

THE OLD WEST: GUNSLINGING BODYGUARDS

THE FRONTIER TOWNS OF THE OLD WEST could be pretty wild and woolly. Places like Dodge City and Tombstone were notorious for shootings and brawls. Marshals and sheriffs had the hard job of keeping law and order. Some of them—Wild Bill Hickok, Wyatt Earp and Bat Masterson, for example—became famous. These lawmen were tough customers and skilled gunfighters. Because they knew how to deal with troublemakers, they were sometimes hired as bodyguards. But not every gunslinging bodyguard was a legendary lawman. Some of them were outlaws.

I CALL SHOTGUN!

Shotgun guards were bodyguards in the Old West. They rode on stagecoaches next to the driver and carried a shotgun to protect the passengers from robbers. The term "riding shotgun" is still used for armed guards who protect people or valuables being transported from one place to another—and by siblings fighting over who gets to ride in the front passenger seat!

WHEN THE ENGLISH JOURNALIST ISABELLA BIRD TRAVELED THROUGH THE AMERICAN WEST, HER BODYGUARD AND GUIDE WAS ROCKY MOUNTAIN JIM NUGENT, A TOUGH CHARACTER WHO HAD A REPUTATION AS A GUNMAN. MISS BIRD HAD NO TROUBLE WHILE SHE WAS UNDER JIM'S WATCHFUL EYE. A FEW MONTHS AFTER THEY PARTED COMPANY, JIM WAS KILLED IN A GUNFIGHT. LATER, ISABELLA CLAIMED THAT SHE'D HAD VISITS FROM HIS GHOST.

IN NEW MEXICO, a rancher named John Tunstall became involved in a range war. He was one of the small ranchers who were fighting for a share of the land against a powerful organization called the Company. The Company was made up of big-time ranchers and their business friends who wanted complete control of the territory. Gunmen and thugs who worked for the Company bullied the small ranchers.

New Mexico at that time was a lawless territory. There wasn't a single lawman Tunstall could turn to. Like most of the people in the Old West, Tunstall wasn't an expert with a gun. It took a lot of practice to learn how to shoot well, and not many people were really good at it. If you had trouble, you hired someone who was.

Tunstall hired several gunmen to work for him as cowboys and bodyguards. One of them was a young man known as Billy Bonney. Billy was a homeless drifter who had already had brushes with the law. He'd been in jail on a charge of stealing some clothes, but he'd escaped by climbing up through the chimney. There were rumors that Billy might even have killed a man in self-defense when he was just sixteen years old. But Billy was a good cowhand—even better, he was good with a gun. He was exactly what Tunstall needed.

Billy was an outlaw, and there were few people he could trust. He was grateful to Tunstall for taking him in and giving him a job. He saw Tunstall as a friend and became fiercely loyal to him.

Billy and his companions went everywhere with Tunstall. The Company thugs kept their distance, because they had heard about Billy's skill with a gun. But they watched for a chance to get at the rancher.

One day Tunstall, Billy, and a few of the other men were driving a small herd of horses to town. Along the way they spotted a flock of wild turkeys. Tunstall told his men to shoot a few of the birds so they could take them back to the ranch for supper. Billy and the others galloped off, whooping and firing their guns. Tunstall stayed with the horses and watched as his bodyguards got farther and farther away from him.

Suddenly a band of mounted Company gunmen appeared. Billy realized that he and his friends were outnumbered. He shouted to Tunstall and the others to ride for the top of a hill. They could take cover behind some big rocks up there and fight off the attackers. As Billy raced up the hill, he assumed Tunstall was right behind him.

The bodyguards reached the hilltop. When Billy looked back, he was dismayed to see that Tunstall was still with the horse herd, alone, unarmed, and unprotected. Billy would never find out why Tunstall didn't ride to safety, because the Company gunmen quickly shot the rancher dead. Then they rode away. But Billy had seen some of their faces, and knew who they were.

Billy had failed to protect his friend and employer. But his loyalty didn't end with Tunstall's murder. He swore he would get revenge.

Over the next few months, Billy Bonney became the central figure in one of the most violent chapters in the story of the Old West. He took part in blazing gun battles. He killed several men, some of them in cold blood, without giving them a chance to defend themselves. He became a fugitive, wanted for murder. A sheriff named Pat Garrett finally tracked Billy down and killed him. The story of the young outlaw bodyguard became the legend of Billy the Kid.

BODYGUARDS IN THE UNDERWORLD

THE UNDERWORLD IS A DARK PLACE of greed and violence. Underworld criminals can't look to the police to protect them from their enemies. Even the toughest of bad guy bosses have always needed the extra defenses of bodyguards.

Most underworld bodyguards are in it for the money. They also like the sense of importance the job gives them. If you're a gangster's bodyguard you have to be extra vigilant, because one mistake could do more than get you fired; it might get you killed.

AL CAPONE was one of the most notorious gangster bosses of them all. He was known as Scarface because of the marks a knife left on his face after a bar fight. But he didn't like that name. He preferred to be called Big Al. In Chicago during the 1920s, Big Al ruled a rich but violent criminal empire. He made millions of dollars through bootlegging (the illegal sale of alcoholic beverages), gambling, and extortion. Hundreds of thugs worked for him.

Big Al wasn't the only crime boss in Chicago. Other gangsters wanted in on the action, too. They fought with Big Al and each other over control of "turf," gangster-speak for territory. Shootings and murders became almost daily events. The worst thing that could happen to a gangster wasn't being captured by the police. It was being captured by enemy gangsters. They might take him for a "one-way ride." That meant they would drive him out to the country, shoot him, and leave his body in a ditch.

Or they might give him "cement overshoes." According to underworld rumors, in that particularly cruel and terrifying form of gangland execution, the victim was forced to stand in a tub of wet cement until it hardened. Then the killers would take him out in a boat and drop him into deep water. The heavy cement took him straight to the bottom.

The shadowy, dangerous, criminal world that deals with drugs, smuggling, and other crimes is called "the underworld" because so much of what happens in it has to be kept out of sight.

Big Al had no problem ordering one-way rides or cement overshoes for other gangsters, but he didn't want anyone ordering them for him. He couldn't very well ask the police for protection, so he surrounded himself with bodyguards. He never went anywhere without them. In a way, it was like being a prisoner. Big Al couldn't walk down a street without a gang of men armed with pistols and machine guns surrounding him. If he went to a restaurant, his bodyguards would make customers dining at nearby tables move somewhere else. If someone knocked on the door of Big Al's office, a bodyguard always answered.

In spite of all Big Al's bodyguards, enemy gangsters still tried hard to "bump him off," the underworld term for murder. One day, Big Al was having lunch in a hotel dining room. Suddenly, gunshots echoed from the street. Everybody, including Big Al, rushed to the window to see what was going on. A bodyguard named Frankie Rio was standing right next to him. When Frankie looked out the window, he realized it was a set-up. A column of eight cars was coming down the street, and they all had machine gun barrels sticking out of the windows. The gunshots had been a ploy to lure Big Al to the window.

Frankie grabbed Big Al and threw him to the floor, covering him with his own body just as the shooters in the first car opened fire. Bullets smashed through the window and sprayed the dining room. They shattered dishes and bottles behind the counter and pock-marked the wall. The screams of terrified people mixed with the thunderous racket of gunfire.

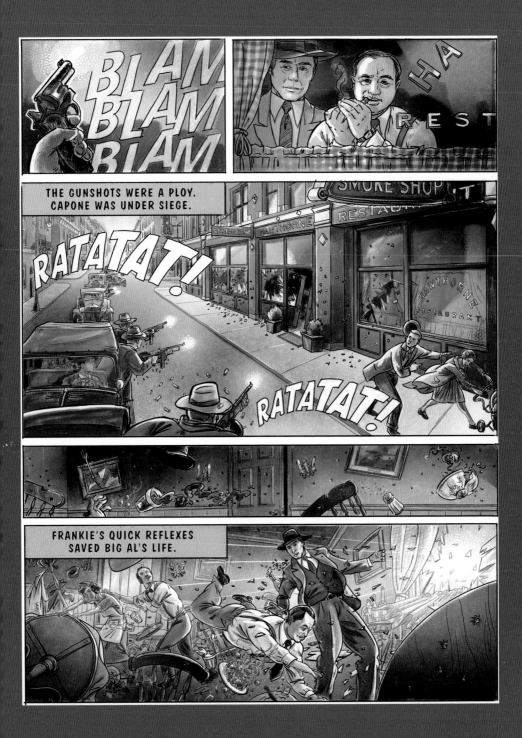

The deafening noise continued as the gunmen in each car took their turns at blasting the front of the hotel. Then the cars sped away, leaving the dining room in a shambles.

Amazingly, nobody was killed. The only ones hurt were two innocent bystanders, a woman whose eye was injured by flying glass, and a little boy whose leg was grazed by a bullet. Big Al didn't have a scratch on him. Frankie's quick action had saved his life. That was good luck for Big Al, if not for law-abiding society.

Of course, Big Al couldn't complain to the police about the attempt on his life. He soon learned that a rival gang boss named Hymie Weiss was behind the attack. Three weeks later, Big Al's gunmen ambushed Weiss and one of his body-guards and bumped them off.

The law eventually caught up with Big Al Capone. A judge sentenced him to a long prison term and Big Al's gangster bodyguards couldn't do a thing about that. By the time he was released from the grim Alcatraz Penitentiary, Big Al was a wreck, physically and mentally. He was no longer a big shot. He was only forty-eight when he died.

DEATH AND TAXES

Al Capone was never tried for murder or any of the other horrific crimes he was involved in. The ruthless gangster was finally convicted and sent to jail on charges of tax evasion.

DRUG LORDS AND BODYGUARDS

IN THE CRIMINAL WORLD TODAY, bootlegging has been
replaced by drug trafficking. Gangs fight each other for turf
where they can sell drugs, just like the gangsters of Al Capone's
day did.

At the top of this deadly business are criminals known
as drug lords. They operate well-organized gangs that deal in
cocaine and other narcotics. But drug-dealing is a cutthroat trade
and a drug lord wouldn't live very long without bodyguards.

One of the most notorious drug lords was Pablo Escobar of
Colombia. He began his life of crime as a car thief and smuggler.
Then he became a bodyguard for a drug dealer and soon discov-
ered that drugs brought in a lot of money.

Escobar set up his own operation and quickly became very
rich from smuggling cocaine into the United States. He had all
his rivals murdered and was soon the biggest drug lord in South
America. He bribed police and government officials, killing the
ones who couldn't be bribed. Of course, Escobar had an army
of bodyguards. He needed them, because he had made a lot of
enemies who wanted him dead.

COLOMBIAN COUNTRY CLUB?

Escobar wasn't sent to an ordinary prison. It was more like a luxury hotel. He was confined, but had all the comforts he wanted. He even continued to run his drug operation from "behind bars."

For years Escobar got away with his crimes. Then the Colombian government began to crack down on the drug lords. Escobar was cornered and agreed to surrender and stop dealing cocaine in return for a light sentence and special treatment.

Meanwhile, Escobar's friends, relatives, and associates came under attack by a vigilante group called Los Pepes. Vigilantes are civilians who take the law into their own hands. The name Los Pepes was taken from *Perseguidos por Pablo Escobar*—"people persecuted by Pablo Escobar." Some of the vigilantes were friends and relatives of Escobar's victims, but many were members of rival drug gangs. Los Pepes killed more than three hundred people connected to Escobar.

Escobar began to worry that Los Pepes might get at him in his comfortable prison. He also worried that the Colombian government might send him to the United States. He knew that if the Americans got their hands on him, he would surely spend the rest of his life in a real prison. Rather than let that happen, he escaped.

Escobar had to go into hiding. He was now being hunted by Colombian police and soldiers, as well as American agents. Bounty hunters were after him for the reward on his head. Most of his bodyguards had abandoned him out of fear of Los Pepes. One of the few who remained loyal was Alvaro de Jesus Agudelo, known as *El Limon* (the Lemon).

El Limon was entrusted with carrying messages between the fugitive drug lord and his family. But on December 2, 1993, Colombian police found Escobar's hideout in the city of Medellin. The arch-criminal who once had dozens of bodyguards at his command now had only one. Escobar and El Limon exchanged gunfire with the police as they ran across the roofs of houses in their attempt to escape. Both of them were shot and killed. The triumphant police officers had their picture taken with Escobar's body. El Limon wasn't a big enough prize for such a photo. He was only a bodyguard who had chosen to be loyal to the wrong man.

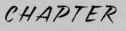

CHAPTER

4

WHEN BODYGUARDS FAIL OR BETRAY

EVEN THOUGH THERE HAVE BEEN BODYGUARDS who are no better than hired thugs protecting bad guys, most bodyguards protect innocent men, women, and children who only want to go about their daily lives without fear. People seldom notice when a bodyguard has done his or her job well. After all, a bodyguard's goal is to make sure that nothing unexpected—especially nothing bad—happens. But bodyguards are only human, and things can and do go wrong. Even when sharp and loyal bodyguards are on the job, mistakes can happen, and those mistakes can have tragic results. We seldom hear about the countless watchful, talented men and women who have kept people safe, but we know a great deal about those who botched the job or were guilty of treachery.

TO KILL A KING

ON MARCH 16, 1792, King Gustavus III of Sweden attended an elegant masquerade ball at the Royal Opera House in Stockholm. The king was in full costume, but the royal silver star pinned to his shirt was a giveaway—one that would prove fatal.

Gustavus was popular with the common people but some of the nobility hated him because of his proposed reforms. They didn't want to lose any of their old aristocratic privileges. The king didn't know that among the guests that evening were three men who wanted to kill him. Two of them, Claes Horn and Adolf Ribbing, were aristocrats. The third was a former member of the King's Guard named Jacob Anckarstrom. He had recently been kicked out of the royal bodyguard for making insulting remarks about the king. Horn and Ribbing used Anckarstrom's intense hatred for Gustavus to their advantage, convincing him to be the key agent in their plot.

The conspirators picked the masquerade ball as the perfect setting for an attack. Everyone would be in disguise and after the deed had been done it would be almost impossible for witnesses to identify the killer—or so the plotters hoped.

The conspirators easily got past the guards at the door. They watched Gustavus closely and waited for the right moment. At his dining table, the king was handed an anonymous letter warning him of the assassination plot, but he ignored it.

Finally, Gustavus finished his meal and stepped onto the ballroom floor. Horn and Ribbing approached him. One of them said, "Good evening. Fine mask."

That was the signal for Anckarstrom. He came up behind the king, pulled out a gun, and shot him in the back. Gustavus collapsed to the floor.

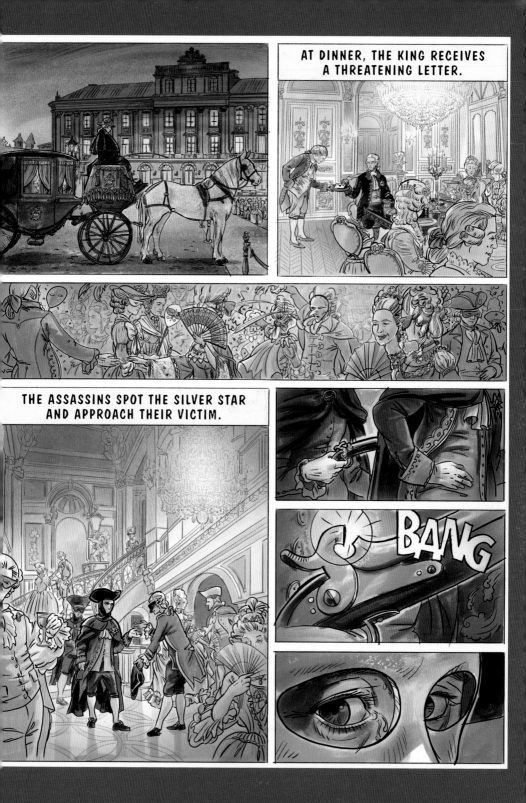

The sound of the shot threw the ballroom into mayhem. Guards blocked the exits, but the assassins had already slipped out.

Somehow, the authorities discovered the identities of the conspirators and Anckarstrom, Ribbing, and Horn were arrested the next day. All three confessed to the crime. Thirteen days after being shot, King Gustavus died of an infection. Because Horn and Ribbing were of the nobility and were seen as mere accomplices in the crime, their punishment was exile. But Anckarstrom, the one who had pulled the trigger, was flogged, his right hand chopped off, and then he was beheaded. Jacob Anckarstrom went down in Swedish history as a villain—a royal bodyguard turned traitor.

— CASE FILE —
RUSSIA, 1918
Murder of a Royal Family

DURING THE RUSSIAN REVOLUTION, COMMUNIST FORCES OVERTHREW TSAR NICHOLAS II. ON JULY 17, 1918, HE AND HIS WIFE, THEIR FOUR DAUGHTERS, AND THE HEIR TO THE THRONE, THIRTEEN-YEAR-OLD PRINCE ALEXEI, WERE ALL SHOT TO DEATH. ONE OF THE GUNMEN WAS ALEXEI KABANOV, A FORMER MEMBER OF THE ROYAL BODYGUARD. KABANOV THOUGHT THAT BY PARTICIPATING IN THE EXECUTION, HE WOULD PROVE HIS LOYALTY TO THE REVOLUTIONARY GOVERNMENT.

VENGEFUL PROTECTORS

IN INDIA'S LONG HISTORY there have been terrible religious conflicts. Some members of the Sikh faith longed to have their part of the country, the Punjab, separate from India to become an independent Sikh nation. That longing turned to fury after the Indian army attacked Sikh separatists in the shrine called the Golden Temple in June 1984.

Prime Minister Indira Gandhi wanted to send a strong message that Sikhs were part of the Indian community, and should not consider breaking away. She included Sikh soldiers in her personal bodyguard to show just how much she trusted them.

Two of her Sikh bodyguards were Satwant Singh and Beant Singh. (They were not related. *Singh* in the Sikh religion means "lion," and is used as a name by all males.) But unbeknownst to the prime minister, Satwant and Beant had no intention of saving Mrs. Gandhi's life—they wanted revenge for the attack on the Golden Temple.

On October 31, 1984, Prime Minister Gandhi left her house to go to her office. The British actor Peter Ustinov was waiting there to interview her for a documentary film. She had to walk through a garden where Satwant and Beant stood guard at a gate. As Mrs. Gandhi passed by, the two men who had been trusted to protect her life turned their guns on her and opened fire. Mrs. Gandhi died on the garden path from multiple gunshot wounds.

Other bodyguards responded immediately. They shot Beant dead and arrested Satwant. He was tried, convicted, and hanged. The bodyguards' act of betrayal only made the religious troubles in India worse.

THE DOUBLE-CROSSER

IN THE CRIMINAL WORLD, bodyguards have been known to betray the person who trusts them most—if the price is right. One such double-crosser was Tony Alescio. Tony was an orphaned immigrant boy from Sicily who arrived in the United States around 1911. At first he lived in Detroit with an uncle who abused him, so although he was very young, Tony ran away. He was taken in by Antonio Giannola, a notorious gangster. Giannola eventually adopted Tony and raised him as his own son. When Tony was old enough, Giannola made him his personal bodyguard.

In early 1919, gangster violence was a big problem in Detroit. Giannola and other gang bosses were fighting for control of the streets. A rival criminal named John Vitale wanted to kill Giannola. But first he had to lure him out into the open. Vitale offered Tony a deal. If he would betray the only father he'd ever known, Vitale would reward Tony with money and a high position in his gang. In spite of everything his adopted father had done for him, Tony accepted Vitale's offer.

First, one of Vitale's gunmen killed a close friend of Giannola's. Giannola went to the dead man's home to pay his respects to the grieving family and, as usual, took Tony with him, trusting that his adopted son would stand by him if there was trouble. Giannola never suspected that when he got out of the car in front of his murdered friend's home, Tony would shoot him dead.

Treacherous Tony hid out in Buffalo for a few months to avoid getting arrested. Then he returned to Detroit to claim his reward from Vitale. But he didn't enjoy it for long. Within a year, Tony Alescio himself was shot and killed.

THE UNGUARDED DOOR

ABRAHAM LINCOLN WAS PRESIDENT of the United States during a time of great crisis in American history. The northern and southern states were divided by many issues, especially slavery, which was still legal in the South but not in the North. From 1861 to 1865, more than six hundred thousand lives were lost in the bloody War Between the States.

President Lincoln didn't like to have bodyguards around him. He worried that the public would think he was afraid. All through the long years of the Civil War, Lincoln had refused to have special protection. Only a few police officers guarded the White House. Lincoln didn't know that at night his close friend Ward Hall Lamon patrolled the White House grounds himself. Lamon tried to make sure that Lincoln was protected, whether the president liked it or not.

On April 9, 1865, the army led by Confederate General Robert E. Lee surrendered, and the bitter Civil War that had caused such terrible bloodshed and sorrow finally ended.

But not every Southerner could accept that the South had lost the war. One of them was an actor named John Wilkes Booth. He decided to kill President Lincoln.

On April 14, Lincoln and his wife Mary were scheduled to go to Ford's Theatre to see a play. Ward Hall Lamon was uneasy. He begged Lincoln to stay home. But Lamon had to go out of town on official business and Lincoln shrugged off his friend's warning.

That night, Mr. and Mrs. Lincoln sat in a special presidential box overlooking the stage. The entrance to the box was supposed to be guarded by a policeman named John F. Parker. He'd been at his post when Lincoln arrived, but he didn't stay there. Instead, he went to a tavern for a drink, leaving the door unguarded.

While Lincoln was enjoying the play, Booth entered the theater. The staff all knew him well because he had often performed there. No one suspected that he had murder on his mind. Booth went to the door that Parker had abandoned, quietly opened it, and crept inside with a pistol in his hand. He shot Abraham Lincoln in the back of the head.

Booth jumped down to the stage and escaped from the theater. He was eventually shot and killed by soldiers. President Lincoln died nine hours after being shot, the first American president to be assassinated. John F. Parker was never punished for leaving his post, but he went down in history as the bodyguard who failed in his duty to protect Abraham Lincoln.

FINAL ORDERS

Only hours before he was assassinated, President Abraham Lincoln gave Secretary of the Treasury Hugh McCulloch official permission to organize a federal agency to fight counterfeiting. That was the first step toward the formation of the U.S. Secret Service.

BAD DAY IN DALLAS

BODYGUARD PROTECTION certainly makes things difficult for would-be attackers. But even the best bodyguards admit that it's impossible to guarantee the safety of a person from somebody who is determined to do harm. They can only do their very best to reduce the danger.

On November 22, 1963, on his way to Dallas, Texas, President John F. Kennedy remarked, "If anybody really wanted to shoot the president of the United States, it's not a very hard job. All that one has to do is get in a high building some day with a telescopic rifle, and there is nothing anybody can do to defend against such an attempt on the president's life."

Kennedy was both right and wrong. Tragically, he was right that shooting the president wouldn't be a very hard job. A few hours after he spoke those words, an assassin shot him as he traveled along a Dallas street in an open car. The Secret Service agents walking alongside the car weren't an effective shield against a sniper's bullets. The investigation concluded that a gunman named Lee Harvey Oswald shot the president from a window in a tall building using a telescopic rifle. But Kennedy was wrong that there was no defense against such an attack.

Part of the problem was that Kennedy wanted the people to see him. That meant riding in an open car instead of a closed one, despite warnings that the president was not popular in Dallas, and that there could be trouble. Kennedy's bodyguards didn't take those warnings seriously enough. Their biggest mistake was in not scouting the route his car would take beforehand, so they could identify and secure danger points such as high windows.

To this day there are many unanswered questions about the assassination of President Kennedy. There are even doubts about who actually shot him. But the fact that his bodyguards failed to protect him resulted in major changes in security protocol for the president of the United States and other important leaders. Motorcade routes are now carefully scouted and secured. The days when presidents were sitting ducks in open cars are over.

— CASE FILE —
DALLAS, 1963
Murder on TV

LEE HARVEY OSWALD WAS ARRESTED A LITTLE OVER AN HOUR AFTER KENNEDY WAS SHOT. TWO DAYS LATER, IN FULL VIEW OF TELEVISION CAMERAS, AS POLICE WERE ABOUT TO TRANSFER HIM FROM THE DALLAS POLICE STATION TO THE COUNTY JAIL, A MAN NAMED JACK RUBY SHOT OSWALD DEAD, SILENCING HIM FOREVER AND LEAVING BEHIND A MYSTERY THAT MIGHT NEVER BE SOLVED.

DEATH OF A PRINCESS

WHEN LADY DIANA SPENCER married Charles, the Prince of Wales, she became the "People's Princess" and one of the best-loved celebrities in the world. Such popularity came at a steep price. Even after the marriage ended in divorce, everywhere Diana went, she was followed by paparazzi who swarmed around her like bees. One of the hardest parts of the celebrity bodyguard's job is keeping the paparazzi away from their client.

On August 31, 1997, Diana and her boyfriend, Emad "Dodi" Fayed, were having dinner at the Hotel Ritz in Paris. It was close to midnight when they finished, but at least thirty paparazzi were waiting in front of the hotel, watching for the famous couple to come out. Some of these photographers were known to hotel security staff as being particularly troublesome. There had already been some scuffles.

To avoid the paparazzi, the couple's security team decided to create a diversion. A few bodyguards drove away in decoy cars parked at the front of the hotel to lure the paparazzi away, while Diana and Dodi went out the back door. The ruse didn't work.

Diana and Dodi got into a black Mercedes-Benz. With them were a bodyguard named Trevor Rees-Jones and Henri Paul, who was head of security at the Ritz. Paul was driving. The others didn't know that he did not have the chauffeur's license required to drive that kind of car. Nor did they realize that he had been drinking. Paparazzi who had gone around to the back of the hotel saw Diana's party get into the Mercedes. Henri Paul taunted them, saying they would have to drive fast to catch him.

The Mercedes roared away, with paparazzi on motorcycles in pursuit. Paul was driving fast. He tried to lose the paparazzi by pulling into the Place de l'Alma underpass. There, Paul lost control of the car and crashed into a pillar. None of the occupants were wearing seatbelts. Diana, Dodi, and Paul were all killed. Rees-Jones survived, but he was seriously injured.

Paparazzi reached the awful scene in the tunnel right after the accident. They continued snapping pictures of the wreck and the victims until police and emergency teams arrived and ordered them away.

An investigation concluded that the deaths had been caused by a combination of Henri Paul's drunk driving, the chase of the paparazzi, and the failure to wear seatbelts. As a security professional, Paul failed his clients by drinking on the job and getting behind the wheel of a car he wasn't qualified to drive. Mohamed Al-Fayed, Dodi's father, also held Trevor Rees-Jones responsible. He said that the bodyguard had failed to do his job properly. Rees-Jones suffered severe head injuries in the accident and cannot remember all the details of what happened that night.

CHAPTER

5

THE HIGH PRICE OF FAME

IN 1932, A KIDNAPPER STOLE THE BABY SON of aviation hero Charles Lindbergh right out of his nursery. All over the world people hoped for his safe return, but the child was eventually found dead. In 1980, former Beatle John Lennon was shot to death in front of his apartment building. The murderer, Mark David Chapman, thought that by killing a celebrity, he would become famous, too. In 1995, Latin singing star Selena was shot and killed in a hotel by the president of her fan club after an argument over money. The Lindbergh family was not protected by bodyguards; neither were John Lennon or Selena. Today almost every celebrity, and would-be celebrity, has at least one bodyguard.

The Canadian teen idol Justin Bieber found that problems can come with sudden stardom. He said, "It's definitely scary when girls are all around me and I can't go anywhere."

NEW YORK, 1980

The Easiest Target

JOHN LENNON'S ASSASSIN HAD THE NAMES OF SEVERAL CELEBRITIES ON A LIST OF POTENTIAL VICTIMS. HE DECIDED THAT LENNON, WHO DID NOT HAVE A BODYGUARD, WOULD BE THE EASIEST TARGET. FOLLOWING LENNON'S MURDER, THE DEMAND FOR CELEBRITY BODYGUARDS ROSE SHARPLY.

GUARDING THE STARS

GUARDING A CELEBRITY may seem glamorous but much of the hard work happens behind the scenes. Bodyguards regularly scan fan letters for threats and hate mail. They create exit plans so that performers can leave the stage and be whisked away while the audience is still applauding. They devise ways to quietly get their clients through airports, in disguise if necessary. In hotels, restaurants, and other public places, bodyguards make sure they know where all the exits are, in case the client needs to make a quick getaway.

THE MEMPHIS MAFIA: GUARDING THE KING OF ROCK & ROLL

CELEBRITY BODYGUARDS are usually hired through agencies that have strict rules and regulations. The bodyguards are expected to treat the celebrities as business clients, nothing more. However, one famous group of bodyguards was an exception.

In 1956, Elvis Presley turned the music world on its ear as the first big star of rock and roll. He had a sensational style that thrilled young people. Teenage admirers all over the world called Elvis the King of Rock and Roll. He had wealth and fame that other entertainers could only dream of.

But Elvis became a prisoner of his own fame. He couldn't go to a movie or even walk down the street because of the hordes of screaming girls. Their jealous boyfriends sometimes wanted to get close enough to Elvis to punch him. In his piles and piles of fan mail were threatening letters from people who thought that he was a bad influence on young people.

Elvis chose his bodyguards from a close circle of friends and relatives. Because he lived in Memphis, Tennessee, they were nicknamed the Memphis Mafia. Elvis didn't like that name, probably because of the criminal association. But the bodyguards thought it gave them a tough image.

BACK OFF!

Movie stars Brad Pitt and Angelina Jolie have asked for laws to be passed to protect the children of celebrities from being harassed by paparazzi.

The Memphis Mafia lived with Elvis in his mansion, Graceland. Elvis's presence would cause a riot if he went out in public, so his bodyguards were on call night and day to do all of the simple things Elvis couldn't do for himself, like shopping. When Elvis traveled, they surrounded him like Secret Service agents around the president. The singer was always afraid that somebody would shoot him when he was on stage, so the Memphis Mafia would circulate through the audience when Elvis was doing a concert. His fame forced him to live in a well-protected, secluded, lonely world. In many ways, the men in the Memphis Mafia were Elvis's only friends.

The public was always hungry for details about Elvis's private life. After he died of a drug overdose in 1977, several former members of the Memphis Mafia wrote articles and books about their lives with the King of Rock and Roll, or fed other writers personal information. Elvis had forbidden his bodyguards to take unauthorized photographs of him or sell confidential information to the press. After his death, did the Memphis Mafia honor Elvis's memory, or did they sell out to fans who wanted every possible tidbit of information?

SLEEPWALKING IN MEMPHIS

Since childhood, Elvis had a chronic sleepwalking problem. To keep him safe, one of the Memphis Mafia often slept in the same room as the musician. The bodyguards also made sure doors and windows were locked so Elvis couldn't get out if he started walking in his sleep.

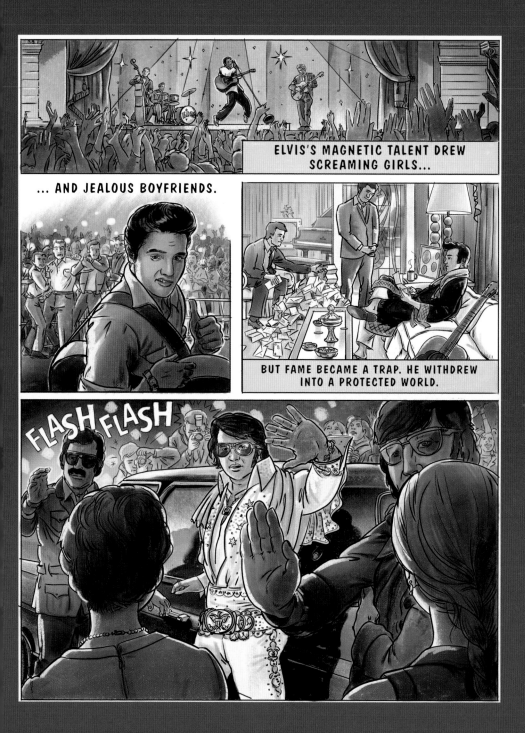

PROTECTION WITH A HEART

ELIJAH SHAW is one of the most successful bodyguards in the world. He is the founder of the security agency Icon Services Corporation and has guarded such stars as Naomi Campbell, Christina Milian, Chris Rock, Chaka Khan, Usher, and 50 Cent. His security people have worked in countries around the world protecting celebrities, corporate executives, and political figures. But not all of the people who've been protected by Icon are rich and famous.

Elijah grew up in a poor neighborhood in Chicago. His mother was a single parent who worked hard to provide for Elijah and his two older brothers. Because of her love and the great example she set, Elijah developed a strong respect for women.

When he was young, Elijah dreamed of becoming a movie director. He went to work as a bodyguard to earn money to put himself through film school but soon discovered that he liked the job. His desire to protect people was stronger than his desire to make movies.

Even after he became successful, Elijah never forgot what it had been like to grow up in poverty. He knew all about the hardships faced by single mothers. One of Elijah's brothers worked in a program that helped abused women and learning of his brother's experiences made Elijah realize that there was a way he could help, too.

Elijah established the ISC Safety Net Program. Icon bodyguards volunteer their services for victims of domestic abuse. Many women who leave an unsafe situation at home do so with little more than the

clothes they are wearing. Often there are children involved, and they could be in danger if left behind. Police can't always give women in these situations the protection they need. That's where Elijah's bodyguards come in.

Free of charge, an Icon bodyguard will escort a woman back to her home so she can collect belongings that she and her children need. Elijah's bodyguards will also make sure that women and children staying in shelters for victims of domestic abuse aren't disturbed or threatened. This protection allows the women to make necessary changes in their lives safely and with dignity. Elijah says it is his way of giving something back to the community.

CHAPTER

6

ON ASSIGNMENT

TED HAD A DANGEROUS JOB TO DO. His company had been losing millions of dollars in its South American office. Somebody was stealing that money and it looked like an inside job. Ted had to travel to South America to solve the mystery. He knew that the embezzlers would stop at nothing, including murder, to get away with their crime. Ted began getting death threats before he even left the United States. Shawn Engbrecht and his team were called in.

Seventeen people worked in that office, but Ted didn't know which ones were embezzlers and which ones were honest. He couldn't trust anybody. It took him four months, working eighteen to twenty hours a day, to finally get to the root of the problem. Twelve people—70 percent of the office management—had been involved in the embezzling scam. They thought the death threats would make Ted too afraid, even if they were caught, to actually do anything to them.

Embezzlers steal money from their employers and then make up phony accounting records to hide the crime.

Shawn's team guarded Ted around the clock while he did his work. They stayed close to him at the office, and they occupied a whole floor of the hotel where he was staying. Once Ted had the evidence and knew who the embezzlers were, the team helped him set up a trap. Everyone in office management was invited to a conference. None of the embezzlers suspected a thing. Shawn's team had even fooled the embezzlers' spies into thinking it was a regular business meeting.

When the office staff gathered in the conference room, none of them knew that Ted was wearing a bulletproof vest under his shirt. The crooks were completely surprised when the bodyguards and some national police officers suddenly poured into the conference room. Ted fired all of the embezzlers immediately and had them escorted off company property. What happened to them after that would be up to that country's government. But that wasn't the end of the story. The angry crooks sent hired killers after Ted. Shawn's team protected him, hiding him until they could get him safely out of the country.

Shawn Engbrecht is a private security contractor for the Center for Advanced Security Studies in the United States. He and his team have taken on "close protection" assignments as top-level bodyguards in trouble spots all over the world, including Iraq and Afghanistan. They are highly paid because the work is extremely dangerous. On the job, bodyguards face every sort of threat you can imagine, from gunmen to deadly snakes. Shawn shares some eye-popping inside information about his work, but he cannot and will not reveal all the details for security reasons and because of the bodyguard's code of trust.

"Close protection" is the phrase bodyguards use to describe what they do to make sure their clients have a safe environment and are able to go about their daily lives without fear.

ASSIGNMENT MEXICO: GUARDING JUAN

WELL-ORGANIZED GANGS OF KIDNAPPERS operating in Mexico have caused much fear and suffering. They target the children of rich and even not-so-rich families and hold them for ransom. The country was outraged by the horrifying case of fourteen-year-old Fernando Marti. Everybody knew that Fernando's family owned a chain of sporting goods stores and that they had a lot of money. On June 8, 2008, Fernando and his bodyguard were being driven to school in an armored car. At a roadblock, a group of armed men wearing police uniforms stopped the car. The men were not police officers, but kidnappers in disguise. The kidnappers killed the chauffeur and strangled the bodyguard. He was dumped on the road and left for dead, but he survived.

— CASE FILE —
VENEZUELA, 2003
Autograph, Please

VERUSKA RAMIREZ, A FASHION MODEL AND FORMER MISS VENEZUELA, WAS ABDUCTED FROM HER CAR BY KIDNAPPERS. THEY ROBBED HER, BUT THEN RELEASED HER THREE HOURS LATER, AFTER SHE AUTOGRAPHED SOME PICTURES FOR THEM.

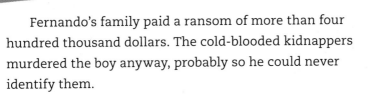

Fernando's family paid a ransom of more than four hundred thousand dollars. The cold-blooded kidnappers murdered the boy anyway, probably so he could never identify them.

Solving such crimes is hard, especially if the police don't have modern, high-tech investigative resources. Even if victims are returned safely to their families after the ransom has been paid, unless the kidnappers are stopped, they'll strike again. Many people hire bodyguards to protect their children, but as the Fernando Marti case showed all too well, sometimes that isn't enough.

When Shawn and his team are assigned to protect a child, they want to do more than just discourage the kidnappers. They want to have the criminals arrested and sent to jail. "We really like to catch those guys," Shawn says.

Let's join Shawn and his team as they use a system of professional surveillance and counter-surveillance to turn the kidnappers' own tricks against them. This training scenario shows us how the bodyguards would handle a similar real-life assignment.

A FAMILY IN MEXICO CITY hires Shawn and his team to protect their young son. We'll call him Juan. They are concerned for the boy's safety, and they're fed up because the whole neighborhood has been terrorized by a gang of kidnappers. They want the gang stopped.

A bodyguard openly escorts Juan everywhere he goes. Meanwhile, other security team members blend into the background, secretly watching. Every day they take pictures of anyone who goes near Juan, or seems to be following him. The bodyguards know that kidnappers study their targets to learn their daily routines and determine the best time and place to snatch them. While the kidnappers have Juan under observation, Shawn's team looks for telltale signs of kidnapper activity, so they can turn the hunters into the hunted.

Day after day, Juan's bodyguards watch people and study photographs. They look for "matches"—faces that keep appearing in multiple shots. They also watch for people who seem to be trying to avoid being noticed by changing their clothing or altering their appearance. The kidnappers are often amateurs at this sort of deception, and professionals can spot them easily. After a thorough study, Shawn's team has convincing evidence that bad guys are indeed stalking Juan. Now they can set a trap for the kidnappers. But they have to use Juan as bait.

The team selects a "choke point." That's a side street or some other location where there aren't many people around. All of the approaches and exits can be monitored. No one can enter the area without being seen.

Escorted by his visible bodyguard, Juan walks through the choke point. The hidden bodyguards watch to see if he is followed by any of the "matches" they have spotted in the photographs. If he is, the team can be pretty sure that they have the kidnappers pegged.

Now the team can turn the tables. Having identified the kidnappers, the team can follow *them* around and collect more information. They might even learn their names and where they live.

When Shawn's team has gathered enough evidence to prove that these people have been stalking Juan, they can ask for help from the police. They will set up a "staging area," a location that appears to be the perfect place for the kidnappers to snatch their victim and make a getaway. Once again, Juan has to be the bait. But when the kidnappers make their move, Shawn's team and a squad of police officers are ready for them. Juan is safe, and the kidnapping gang is headed for jail.

A BODYGUARD'S WORK BOOK

RULE #1: THE FIRST PRIORITY

IN CASES LIKE JUAN'S, Shawn's team use a combination of brains, brawn, and technology to be "proactive," which means getting prepared before anything bad can happen. It is considered the best trick of the trade because it is much better than being "reactive," responding *after* something bad has happened. The bodyguard's first priority is to avoid trouble. Planning, therefore, is vital to a successful close protection assignment.

THE BODYGUARD'S CHECKLIST

1 Keep the client in sight at all times.
2 Check that all sites where the client will be (home, car, office) are secure.
3 Scout travel routes and avoid danger spots.
4 Prepare alternative routes in case of an emergency.
5 Keep an eye out for suspicious-looking people.

RULE #2: HANDS, EYES, AND COMMUNICATIONS

GOOD COMMUNICATION IS ESSENTIAL to a bodyguard team. A bodyguard patrolling a crowd is constantly on the lookout for any sign of a weapon. A person whose hands can't be seen arouses suspicion. If the person's hands are in their pockets or covered by a folded coat or newspaper, they could have a gun. The bodyguard also watches people's eyes to determine if they pose a threat. A suspect's eyes might seem to be *too* focused on the client. Or they might be glancing around nervously, perhaps checking to see if anyone is watching.

If the bodyguard spots a suspicious-looking person, he or she immediately contacts the team by radio or text. The message will start with something like, "I have a problem." The bodyguard will quickly direct the team's attention to the suspect. If the suspect makes a threatening move, the team takes immediate action.

ON THE CLOCK

One method that bodyguards use when escorting a client on foot is called the clock. Each member of the team surrounding the client has a position matching a number on the face of an imaginary clock. If one of them shouts "Gun, five o'clock!" the others know exactly where to look. If the danger point is above eye level, such as an upper-storey window, the bodyguard will shout, "Gun, five o'clock high!"

Sometimes bodyguards who patrol crowds have tiny cameras in their eyeglasses or coat buttons. This is a surveillance trick that helps them secretly record potential troublemakers. Because quick communication is important, bodyguards don't talk over their radios unless absolutely necessary. In an emergency, every second counts, so they don't want the channels tied up with idle talk. To prevent anyone from listening in, they use radios that jump to different frequencies every few seconds.

If there is an actual attack, the bodyguard's first duty is to get the client out of the danger zone. The team members nearest to the client do whatever it takes: hustle him out of the room, shove him to the floor, or push him into a car. The team member nearest to the attacker uses his skills to disarm and subdue him. Even if a bodyguard gets hurt during the action, the team's first duty is still to protect the client.

— CASE FILE —
MEMPHIS, 1968
Deadly Ambush

BECAUSE HE WAS A LEADER IN THE FIGHT FOR CIVIL RIGHTS, MARTIN LUTHER KING, JR. HAD MANY ENEMIES. HE AND HIS BODYGUARDS COURTED DANGER BY ALWAYS USING THE SAME HOTELS AND MOTELS AS THEY TRAVELED AROUND THE COUNTRY. ON APRIL 4, 1968, IN MEMPHIS, TENNESSEE, KING WAS SHOT AND KILLED WHILE HE STOOD ON THE BALCONY OF HIS ROOM AT THE LORRAINE MOTEL. THE ASSASSIN KNEW EXACTLY WHERE HE WAS GOING TO BE.

RULE #3: KEEP 'EM GUESSING

AN IMPORTANT KEY to the bodyguard's defense system is to keep possible attackers from knowing exactly what is going on. The less attackers know about where their target is and what he or she is doing, the better. It's the same defense method China's First Emperor used in his palace. Bodyguards don't let their clients have set routines. Often, if an important client has to travel by car, the bodyguards will arrange a motorcade. Only a few people know which car the client is in. The other cars carry bodyguards who are ready to spring into action at the first sign of trouble.

Throughout history, people responsible for defending themselves and others have come up with ingenious ways to keep potential enemies guessing. Doorways in castles were low, so that an attacker had to bend over to pass through, presenting his head to the swordsman waiting on the other side. Stairways inside castle towers were narrow and built in such a way that an intruder climbing up the stairs had the wall on his right. That gave him very little room to use his sword. Since most people are right-handed, the defender looking down the stairs had an advantage. He had open space to his right, and free use of his sword arm.

In Japan, buildings like Nijo Castle in Kyoto were equipped with "nightingale floors." These floors were deliberately made so that they squeaked when someone walked on them. If the occupant heard the floor "sing like a nightingale," he knew he had an intruder. In frontier America, hunters and trappers used a similar device. They would surround their camp with a system of little bells on strings. If an intruder tripped a string in the dark, the bells would tinkle a warning. The person on guard duty could then awaken the others.

LESSONS LEARNED

For many famous people, secrecy about their travel and accommodation arrangements is important to their security. The bodyguards for superstars like Elvis Presley and the Beatles had the biggest problems with crowds when they were on tour, because people knew in advance where they were going to be. Their experiences were lessons for the bodyguards of future celebrities.

RULE #4: BRING IN THE REINFORCEMENTS
A BEAST, BIRDS, AND OTHER CRITTERS

BODYGUARDS HAVE ALWAYS USED reinforcements—ranging from space-age bulletproof vests and cars to equally inventive, but low-tech measures that may surprise you. Here are some of a bodyguard's best allies.

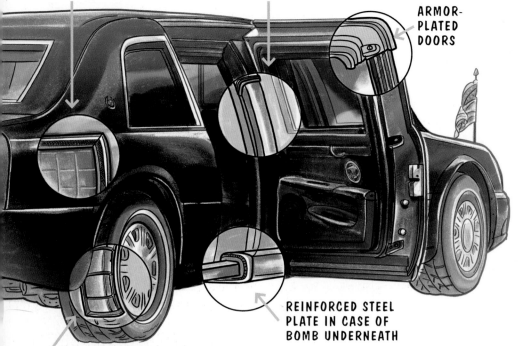

GAS TANK FILLED WITH
SPECIAL FOAM SO IT
WON'T EXPLODE

BODY MADE OF STEEL,
ALUMINUM, TITANIUM,
AND CERAMIC

ARMOR-
PLATED
DOORS

REINFORCED STEEL
PLATE IN CASE OF
BOMB UNDERNEATH

KEVLAR-LINED TIRES
WITH STEEL RIMS

THE BEAST

The Beast is the nickname U.S. Secret Service agents have given to the official limousine the president uses. It is a state-of-the-art, high-tech armored car. It was built to withstand bullets, bombs, and gas. The tires are specially made so that the Beast can keep going even if the tires are flattened. The Beast can fire smoke grenades as a defensive measure and it has a video system that allows the driver to see his way through the smoke. A communications system keeps the president and the bodyguards who ride with him in contact with other government officials and Secret Service agents at all times. In the Beast's trunk there is even a blood bank containing the president's blood type. Only specially trained agents can drive the Beast because armored cars are very heavy, which makes them difficult to drive.

DANGER! GUARD GEESE ON DUTY

The use of animals as bodyguards goes back to ancient times. In Egypt, the pharaoh's bodyguards used trained baboons for crowd control. Baboons are strong, vicious, and have sharp teeth. People would quickly scatter before a guard with a few snarling baboons straining at their leashes.

Geese, which are especially noisy when disturbed, were often a village's alarm system. Aggressive and territorial, geese will attack anyone or anything they think is trespassing on their territory. Even without teeth, their hard bills can give nasty bites. If the geese sensed enemies creeping up in the night, they would make a racket and alert the villagers. A flock of noisy geese once warned the ancient Romans of a surprise night attack by their enemies the Gauls. In some rural areas people still use geese as guard animals.

FIERCE FELINES

Nearly all ancient Egyptians kept cats in their homes for protection. Cats killed rats, and even poisonous snakes like cobras. The Egyptians also believed cats had magical powers that protected homes and children from evil. An Egyptian goddess called Mafdet, known as Avenger of the King, was portrayed with a woman's body and the head of a cheetah or leopard. Another Egyptian cat goddess, named Bast, was known as the Pharaoh's Protector.

Donkeys and llamas have also been used for protection. Both have sensitive hearing and can be trained to sound warnings, and even attack intruders. In Africa and Australia, ostriches, emus, and kangaroos have been trained to protect livestock and keep trespassers off private property.

Of course, dogs have been used for protection for thousands of years, all around the world. Barking dogs warned people in Native American villages of enemy attacks. The ancient Egyptians, Greeks, and Romans all used dogs as guard animals. In some Egyptian tombs, archaeologists have found mummified guard dogs. One of the oldest known dog breeds, the chow chow, did guard duty in ancient China.

Guard dogs are still used everywhere to protect the homes of wealthy and important people. Specially trained dogs are useful at sniffing out explosives that humans might miss. Bodyguards will sometimes have a dog go through a room to make sure it is "clean" before the client enters. Guard dogs are also an especially important part of security in Third World countries where crime rates are high because of poverty.

People usually associate guard dogs with breeds like the German shepherd, Doberman pinscher, and rottweiler. That's because those dogs are big and can overpower a human being. But smaller breeds such as terriers have also been used as guard dogs because they make a lot of noise if they sense an intruder.

Usually the noise the dogs make is enough to scare the trespasser away. But some dogs have had their vocal cords altered so they can't bark. That means they attack silently. A very unpleasant surprise for the intruder!

CHAPTER

7

SO YOU WANT TO BE A BODYGUARD

MOST REAL-LIFE BODYGUARDS are not movie heroes, expert at everything from martial arts to marksmanship. But professional bodyguards are highly trained people who have devoted themselves to a job that brings with it a lot of satisfaction.

If you decide that personal protection is the career for you, the first question you may be asked is, Why do you want to be a bodyguard? You'll need to have a good answer if you're applying to a reputable bodyguard school. Shawn Engbrecht of the Center for Advanced Security Studies says that top-rated bodyguard schools screen applicants carefully. They don't want bullies or people who think they are going to be like James Bond. Successful applicants show self-confidence, respect for others, a good attitude, and a desire to learn. Most important, they understand that real bodyguard work is all about helping other people by keeping them safe.

There was a time when a bodyguard simply had to be big, tough, and male. The job required little, if any, formal education. If you could crack heads, you could be a bodyguard.

In the twenty-first century, however, things are dramatically different. Bodyguard agencies and their clients want people with a good education because in the modern personal protection business, brains are just as important as brawn. They want people who are smart, can think on their feet, and will be a reliable part of a team.

BACK TO SCHOOL

THERE ARE SKILLS A BODYGUARD MUST HAVE, and there are schools that teach them. Top-rated schools like the Center for Advanced Security Studies have courses that last up to twenty-nine days. Training days can be twelve to fourteen hours long, and they can be demanding. Lots of people drop out of the program before it's over. Students who stick with it learn self-defense techniques, firearms skills, and evasive driving. They take courses that involve classroom work and exercises "in the field," the real world outside the classroom. That's where students learn how to use those cool electronic surveillance and communication devices.

Instructors demonstrate how to do the advance scouting that's part of the job. They even teach students the right way to walk with a client. Above all, the instructors stress the importance of using common sense. Clients don't want show-offs for bodyguards. A bodyguard can

NO STUNTMEN REQUIRED

Not many bodyguards find themselves in situations where they have to rappel down cliffs, jump out of airplanes, or leap barriers on motorcycles. That's strictly for the movies.

be faced with all kinds of different emergencies, so learning life-saving skills such as first aid and cardiopulmonary resuscitation (CPR) is as important as learning how to disarm an attacker. It is also important to learn the laws that concern bodyguards. You wouldn't want to be arrested for making a mistake on the job.

Professional bodyguards advise young people just starting out to avoid so-called bodyguard schools that try to attract applicants with images that suggest a career of action and adventure. Those schools take your money and don't train you properly. Beware of bodyguard schools that advertise "revolutionary training techniques" that supposedly teach you all you need to know in a week. There are no shortcuts.

Though you must be in good health and top physical condition to be a bodyguard, you don't necessarily have to be a hulking giant. Most bodyguards today are average-sized and, in fact, more and more women are also choosing this demanding profession.

FEMALE BODYGUARDS

THE IDEA OF FEMALE BODYGUARDS ISN'T NEW.
Greek mythology is full of stories about women warriors called Amazons. Female gladiators fought in ancient Rome. In Scandinavia during the time of the Vikings, women known as shield-maidens served as guards and warriors.

In the early twentieth century, suffragettes were women fighting for the right to vote. Their marches and demonstrations were often broken up by police and gangs of angry men. A British suffragette named Edith Margaret Garrud had learned a form of martial arts called jujutsu. She taught it to a group of thirty other women who formed the secret Bodyguard Society. In several confrontations, the Jujutsuffragettes, as they later came to be known, protected the protesting women from attack and arrest.

Bodyguards are forbidden to use excessive force unless absolutely necessary. A celebrity bodyguard, for example, can block the way of paparazzi, and tell them to back off, but he can't use physical force. If a situation escalates, the bodyguard can only use as much force as is necessary to protect the client. He can't beat anybody up. If the bodyguard doesn't obey the law, he can be charged.

Today, the U.S. Secret Service actively recruits women as agents. An international academy called ATHENA trains women to be bodyguards. In South Korea, one of the leading personal security agencies is the all-female Bluebird Bodyguard Team.

In some situations, female bodyguards have an advantage. Would-be attackers don't suspect them, because they usually expect bodyguards to be male. Women bodyguards can therefore provide a security team with an element of surprise. Many women who need close protection prefer to have female bodyguards because there are "women only" places where men can't go, like change rooms and bathrooms. Some female clients also like the fact that women bodyguards are less of an intrusion on their privacy and aren't as conspicuous in public places.

Not all clients of female bodyguards are women. Among some of the famous men who have had female bodyguards are former New York mayor Rudy Giuliani, England's Prince William, and Indian cricket star Mahendra Singh Dhoni. In fact, Dhoni has an entire squad of armed female bodyguards to protect him from the hordes of hysterical fans who try to mob him everywhere he goes.

Amidst all of the pageantry of the royal wedding of Prince William and Kate Middleton there was very heavy security. Soldiers and police guarded strategic locations, footmen on the royal wedding carriage had guns hidden in their uniforms, and secret service agents mingled with the cheering crowds. In the car that brought Kate to Westminster Abbey was a woman who looked like a member of the wedding party, except she had a gun tucked into her wedding-day finery. She was Emma Probert, Kate's personal bodyguard. If an attacker managed to get past all the other security, Emma was the bride's last line of defense.

One of the world's most famous female bodyguard units was that of former Libyan dictator Muammar Gaddafi. Before Libyan rebels overthrew his regime and killed him in 2011, Gaddafi had between two and three hundred women protectors he called his Amazonians. Forty of them were on duty at any given time, and they accompanied Gaddafi everywhere he went. They were said to be well trained in the use of deadly weapons and were dedicated to defending Gaddafi with their lives. Some people say that Gaddafi's Amazonians were more for show than anything else. And after Gaddafi's regime fell, some former bodyguards came forward to say they were coerced into service and abused. However, in 1998, Libyan rebels opened fire on Gaddafi's motorcade. A bodyguard named Aisha threw herself on top of Gaddafi and was shot several times. She died, and seven other female bodyguards were wounded. Gaddafi escaped with minor injuries.

In 2007, Major Erica Bridge became the first woman to command the 350-year-old King's Troop, the personal protection unit for Queen Elizabeth II.

GADDAFI'S ELITE AMAZONIANS FASCINATED THE WORLD.

ON A DRIVE BY THE SEA, REBELS OPENED FIRE.

POCA POCA POCA

AISHA, THE DICTATOR'S FAVORITE, SACRIFICED HER LIFE.

CASE FILE
IRAQ, 2007
Massacre in Baghdad

THE WAR IN IRAQ BECAME BIG BUSINESS FOR PRIVATE MILITARY CONTRACTOR (PMC) COMPANIES. DAILY VIOLENCE IN CITIES LIKE BAGHDAD MEANT THAT BODYGUARDS WERE IN GREAT DEMAND. MANY OF THE PMCS WERE WELL-TRAINED PEOPLE WHO WORKED ACCORDING TO A PROFESSIONAL CODE OF ETHICS. BUT SOME WERE LITTLE MORE THAN HIRED GUNS WHO USED ANY EXCUSE TO SHOOT AND WHO WERE RESPONSIBLE FOR MANY CIVILIAN CASUALTIES. THE MOST NOTORIOUS INCIDENT WAS THE BLACKWATER MASSACRE OF SEPTEMBER 16, 2007. AMERICAN PMCS ALLEGEDLY OPENED FIRE ON A CROWD, KILLING SEVENTEEN PEOPLE AND WOUNDING TWENTY-FOUR.

ON THE JOB

TRAINING IS OVER and now you are a certified professional bodyguard. Your agency has assigned you a client. She is a corporate executive who works for a global company that has been in the news because of problems involving one of its foreign factories. There have been threats against the company, so all of its senior management personnel have been assigned bodyguards.

You arrive at the client's home before 7:00 a.m. You're wearing a business suit that will help you blend in with the client's work environment. You've taken a colleague's advice and put on good, comfortable shoes, because you're going to be on your feet for most of the day. You won't be able to function well if your feet hurt.

While the client is under your protection, you will be her driver. Before either of you gets into her car, you inspect it to make sure it was not tampered with during the night. Car bombs have become especially tricky because they no longer require wires or timing devices to set them off. A bomb can be detonated by someone using a cell phone a short distance away. You also check to make sure the car's braking system hasn't been sabotaged.

When you set out for the client's office, you don't follow her usual route. You use different routes every day, with no set pattern. You also vary the times of day that you leave the client's home. That makes it difficult for enemies to set up an ambush. While you are driving, you keep an eye on the rearview mirror for any vehicle that seems to be following you. In your training you learned how to spot a vehicle that always seemed to be a few cars behind you no matter where you were.

At the client's office building you turn the car over to an attendant, who will park it in the underground garage.

PROTECTION TO A T

Some celebrity bodyguards have become famous celebrities themselves. Mr. T (formerly Laurence Tureaud) was one of the highest paid bodyguards in the United States. His clients included such stars as martial arts legend Bruce Lee and singer Michael Jackson. He became a star himself, acting in movies and the popular '80s TV show *The A-Team*.

You don't want the client going down there because of the possibility of a trap. As you and the client approach the main door of the building, you make a mental note of a green van at a nearby intersection. During the drive to the office you'd spotted a van just like it in the rearview mirror. Could it be the same one? Unfortunately, it's too far away for you to be able to make out the license plate.

In the front lobby, you and the client both check in at a security guard's desk. The client has a pass card for a private elevator, so you don't have to worry about riding up to her tenth-floor office with strangers. If you did have to use a public elevator, you know a few tricks that would foil any attempt to turn the elevator into a trap. You also know better than to use the stairway, which can be just as potentially dangerous as the underground garage.

Once you reach the client's office, you have to ensure you're not in the way while she does her work. There isn't much for you to do but watch and wait. This is one of the most difficult parts of a bodyguard's job. You have to remain alert in a situation that most other people would find dreadfully boring.

While your client is in a meeting, you look out her window and see a green van parked on the street below. Is it the same one you've seen twice already? Does it pose a threat? You have to check every possibility. You call your agency and report it. Someone will take a close look at the van, get the license number, and investigate further.

At the end of your client's workday, you both go back down to the front of the building. The parking attendant has the car waiting. You give the car another check-over in case anyone managed to breach the garage's security. As you drive down the street, you pass the parked green van. In your rearview mirror, you see it start to pull out from the curb. Suddenly a delivery truck comes along and stops right beside the van, blocking it in. The van driver blasts his horn, but you know that the delivery truck isn't going to move right away. That's because it isn't really a delivery truck. Its driver is from your agency. Your colleagues found enough information about the van to make them suspicious. The driver hasn't broken any laws, so they can't have him arrested. But they can prevent him from following you anymore today. By the time that delivery truck moves, you and your client will be well out of sight. Whoever had been following you won't know that instead of taking your client home, you are taking her to the airport. You're going to accompany her to an important conference in another city, and the enemy won't even know where she's gone. You've done your job well.

HONK! HONK!

DEBRIEF

YOU HAVE COME TO THE END of this journey through the amazing history of bodyguards. From Caesar's armor-clad Praetorian Guard to the technologically advanced agents of the U.S. Secret Service, bodyguards have played a vital and timeless role. King Leonidas's three hundred Spartans and Pope Clement VII's Swiss Guards died heroically in the line of duty. Clietus saved the life of a man who would change the world. The Memphis Mafia added an intriguing chapter to the legend of Elvis Presley. Secret Service agent Larry Buendorf thwarted a would-be assassin's attempt to kill President Ford.

But the story of bodyguards does not end here. Even as you read this, bodyguards are on duty all over the world. They protect heads of state, royalty, and diplomatic figures. Corporate executives in high-risk situations travel in the company of bodyguards. Celebrities rely on bodyguards to keep the paparazzi at bay. In countries where kidnapping is rampant, bodyguards escort children to and from school. Wherever people are in need of extra protection, bodyguards are on the job, making sure their clients can live their lives without fear.

GLOSSARY

AGENCY	→	Most bodyguards work for private agencies that assign them to specific clients.
CLEAN	→	A room that is free of electronic listening devices and other forms of spy technology is said to be "clean."
CLIENT	→	A person or a company a bodyguard has been assigned to protect.
CLOSE PROTECTION	→	What bodyguards provide to make sure their clients have a safe environment and are able to live as normal a life as possible.
CODE OF TRUST	→	A bodyguard has a professional responsibility to never betray a client. The bodyguard must never sell or give away pictures or information that could be harmful or embarrassing to the client.
DANGER SPOT	→	Any location that might be unusually dangerous to a client (e.g., an underground garage).
ELECTRONIC SURVEILLANCE	→	The use of cameras, listening devices, and other technological equipment to spy on someone or to protect an area from intruders.
EVASIVE DRIVING	→	A skill that enables a driver to avoid being followed.

EXIT PLAN	→	A plan made in advance to get a client out of any given place in case of trouble (e.g., knowing the back way out of a hotel or restaurant).
IN THE FIELD	→	The real world, as opposed to the classroom. A bodyguard on an actual assignment is "in the field."
PRIVATE SECURITY CONTRACTOR (PSC)	→	A professional bodyguard who provides protection or security training for individual clients, corporations, and even foreign governments. A PSC often has a police or military background.
SABOTAGE	→	To deliberately damage something in order to harm a person (e.g., tampering with a car's brakes).
SCOUTING	→	Checking out a route in advance to find and secure danger spots.
SECURE AREA	→	A room or any other area that is clean of electronic surveillance devices, and well guarded against intruders.
STALK	→	To follow or watch a person over a period of time for the purpose of kidnapping or some other harmful act.
VISIBLE AND INVISIBLE BODYGUARDS	→	Visible bodyguards are conspicuous. They stand out in a crowd and are meant to deter anyone who would harm a client. Invisible bodyguards blend in with a crowd while they watch for anyone who might pose a threat to the client.

BODYGUARDS THROUGH THE AGES

1570 BCE	Egyptian hieroglyphs tell story of Ahmose, the pharoah's loyal bodyguard
1278 BCE	Ramses II defeats the Sherden sea pirates
480 BCE	Battle of Thermopylae—Immortals vs. Spartans
387 BCE	Geese warn Romans of impending attack from the Gauls
334 BCE	Clietus saves Alexander, and the course of history
210 BCE	Terra Cotta Army escorts First Emperor into afterlife
70 BCE	Gladiators rented out as bodyguards for the rich
27 BCE	Caesar Augustus creates the Imperial Praetorian Guard
900 CE	Viking shield-maidens serve as bodyguards
1506	Pope Julius II hires Swiss mercenaries for protection
1601	Squeaky "nightingale floors" installed in Nijo Castle, Japan
1702	Asano's loyal samurai avenge his death
1792	Bodyguard assassinates King Gustavus of Sweden

APRIL 14 1865	Abraham Lincoln's bodyguard leaves his post
1878	The legend of Billy the Kid is born
1890	Nausica, member of African royal bodyguard, dies a heroic death
JULY 17 1918	Former member of royal bodyguard betrays Tsar Nicholas and family
1919	Rogue bodyguard Tony Alescio kills his adoptive father
1926	Frankie Rio saves Al Capone's life
1933	Hitler's SS is formed
1956	The Memphis Mafia protect the King of Rock & Roll
SEPT 5 1975	U.S. Secret Service saves President Gerald Ford
OCT 31 1984	Bodyguards assassinate Indira Gandhi
DEC 2 1993	Drug lord Pablo Escobar and his bodyguard El Limon killed by Colombian police
AUG 31 1997	Death of Princess Diana
2006	Elijah Shaw launches ISC Safety Net Program
JAN 2009	High-tech armored car nicknamed The Beast comes into presidential service
JUNE 2009	U.S. Secret Service sets up international task force to fight cybercrime

BIBLIOGRAPHY

Bull, George. *Inside the Vatican*. New York: St. Martin's Press, 1982.

Cartledge, Paul. *Alexander the Great: The Hunt for a New Past*. New York: The Overlook Press, 2004.

———. *Thermopylae: The Battle that Changed the World*. New York: Vintage Books, 2007.

Engbrecht, Shawn. *America's Covert Warriors: Inside the World of Private Military Contractors*. Washington, D.C: Potomac Books, 2011.

Escobar, Roberto. *The Accountant's Story*. New York: Grand Central Publishing, 2009.

Gregory, Martyn. *Diana: The Last Days*. London: Virgin Publishing Ltd., 1999.

Horan, James D. *The Authentic Wild West: The Gunfighters*. New York: Crown Publishers, 1976.

Jones, David E. *Women Warriors in History*. London: Brassey's, 1997.

Keefe, Rose. *Guns and Roses*. Nashville, TN: Cumberland House, 2003.

Kessler, Ronald. *In the President's Secret Service*. New York: Crown Publishers, 2009.

King, James A. *Providing Protective Services*. International Association of Personal Protection Agents Inc., Brighton, TV, 1997.

Meltzer, Milton. *In the Days of the Pharaohs*. New York: Franklin Watts (Scholastic), 2001.

Moorhouse, Roger. *Killing Hitler*. New York: Bantam Books, 2006.

Turnbull, Stephen. *Samurai: the Story of Japan's Great Warriors*. London: PRC Publishing, 2004.

Victor, Robert. *The Elvis Encyclopedia*. New York: Overlook Duckworth, 2008.

White, Ronald C. A. *Lincoln: A Biography*. New York: Random House, 2009.

Wood, Frances. *China's First Emperor and His Terra Cotta Warriors*. New York: St. Martin's Press, 2007.

INDEX

A

Adolf Hitler Bodyguard 37–38
Ahmose 4
ahosi 33
Aisha (Gaddafi bodyguard)
   106–107
Alescio, Tony 64–65
Alexander the Great 10, 12–14
Amazonians 106–107
Anckarstrom, Jacob 60–62
animals as bodyguards 97–99
Asano 23
ATHENA 105
Augustus (Emperor of Rome) 17

B

Beast, the 96
Benin *see* Dahomey
Bieber, Justin 75
Bird, Isabella 47
Blackwater Massacre (Iraq) 108
Bluebird Bodyguard Team 105
bodyguard checklist 90
bodyguard schools 101–103
Bonney, Billy (Billy the Kid) 48–49
Booth, John Wilkes 67–68
Braves of the King 6–7
Bridge, Erica 106
Buendorf, Larry 40–41, 113
bushido 21

C

Caligula 18
Capone, Al 50–54, 55
Center for Advanced Security
   Studies 85, 101
Charles V (Holy Roman Emperor)
   35
China, Chinese 26, 30, 98
Clement VII (Pope) 35, 113
Clietus 12–13, 113
Clinton, Bill 42
Companions, the 12

D

Dahomey 31, 33
daimyo 19, 23
Diana, Princess of Wales 71–73

E

Egypt, Egyptians 4, 6, 7, 97, 98
El Limon (Alvaro de Jesus Agudelo) 57
Engbrecht, Shawn 83–85, 87–88, 90, 101
Escobar, Pablo 55–57

F

Fayed, Emad "Dodi" 71–73
female bodyguards 104–106 *see also*
   Minos
First Emperor *see* Qin
Ford, Gerald 40–42, 113
Fromme, Lynette 40–41

G

Gaddafi, Muammar 106–107
Galba (emperor of Rome) 19
Gandhi, Indira 63–64
Garrud, Edith Margaret 104
Germany, Germans 37–39
Giannola, Antonio 64–65
gladiators 15–17
Greece, Greeks 8–11, 98
Gustavus III (king of Sweden) 60–62

H

Henry VIII (king of England) 25
Himmler, Heinrich 38–39
Hitler, Adolf 37–39
Hitler Youth 38
Honourable Band of Gentleman
   Pensioners 25
Horn, Claes 60–62

I

Icon Services Corporation 80–81
Immortals 8, 10–11
ISC Safety Net Program 80–81

J

Japan, Japanese 19, 21, 23, 94
Jujutsuffragettes 104
Julius II (Pope) 34
Julius Caesar 1, 17

K

Kabanov, Alexei 62
katana (samurai sword) 20–21
Kennedy, John F. 69–70
King, Martin Luther, Jr. 93
Kira 22–23

L

Lamon, Ward Hall 66
Lennon, John 75, 76
Leonidas (king of Sparta) 9–11, 113
Lincoln, Abraham 66–68
Lindbergh, Charles 75
Los Pepes 56–57

M

Marti, Fernando 86–87
Memphis Mafia 77–79, 113
Middleton, Kate 106
Minos 31–33

N

Nausica 33
Nazis 37–38
Nicholas II (tsar of Russia) 62
nightingale floors 94–95
ninja 20
Nugent, Jim 47

O

Oswald, Lee Harvey 69–70

P

paparazzi 71–73, 77, 105
Parker, John F. 67–68
Paul, Henri 72–73
Pensioner William 31
Persia, Persians 8, 10–12
pharaohs 4–7, 97
Praetorian Guards 1, 17–19, 113
Presley, Elvis 77–79, 94, 113
Private Military Contractors 108

Probert, Emma 106

Q

Qin (First Emperor of China) 26–30, 93

R

Ramses II 8
Rees-Jones, Trevor 72–73
Ribbing, Adolf 60, 62
riding shotgun 46
Rio, Frankie 52–54
Rome, Romans 15–19, 34, 98
ronin 21–23

S

samurai 1, 19–23
Secret Service *see* United States Secret
    Service
seppuku 21, 23
Shaw, Elijah 80–81
Sherden 8
shoguns 19, 23
Singh, Beant 63–64
Singh, Satwant 63–64
Sparta, Spartans 9–11, 113
SS (*Schutzstaffel*) 37–39
Swiss Guard *see* Vatican Swiss Guard

T

Terra Cotta Army 26–30
Thermopylae 8, 10–11
Tunstall, John 47–49

U

United States Secret Service 40–43, 69,
    96, 105, 113

V

Vatican Swiss Guard 34–36, 113

W

Weiss, Hymie 54
William, Prince 105, 106

X

Xerxes (king of Persia) 8, 10–11
Xi'an 28

IMAGE CREDITS

About the Author and Illustrator

ED BUTTS loved history and adventure stories as a kid, and started writing short stories, articles, and poetry in his teens. On the rare occasions when a magazine published his work, he was overjoyed, especially when they sent him a cheque for ten dollars.

Since then Ed has written books about explorers, adventurers, criminals, hidden treasure, disasters, mysteries, and daring women. He has also worked at many other jobs, including teaching at a school in the Dominican Republic for eight years.

Ed lives in Guelph, Ontario, with his daughter and six-year-old grandson.

SCOTT PLUMBE has camped inside an ancient Roman amphitheater, trekked around Mount Kailash in Tibet, and walked to the source of the Ganges River in India. He has traveled in many countries, including Egypt, Syria, Iran, Morocco, and Japan, which gave him rich experiences to draw on while illustrating the stories in *Bodyguards!*

When he's not painting at his desk in Vancouver, British Columbia, Scott can often be found with his wife and young son in the local Chinese gardens, or sipping tea and planning their next trip.

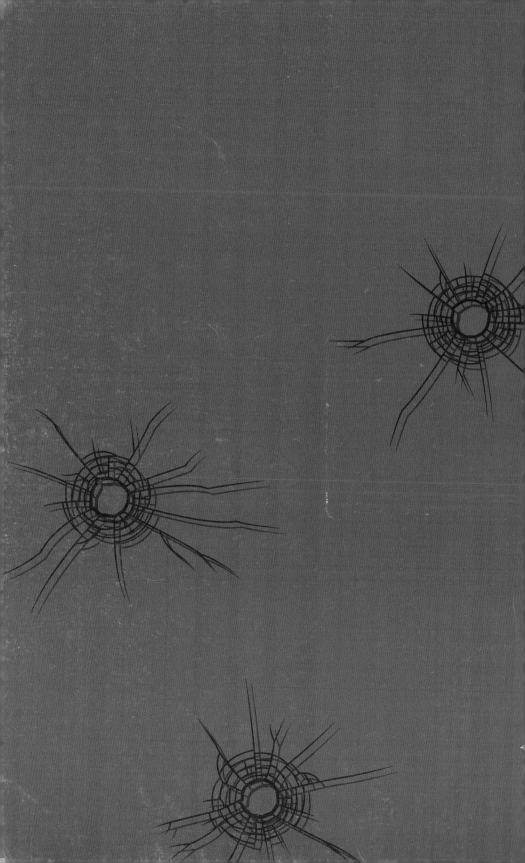